THE SOCIAL BASIS OF RELIGION

THE
SOCIAL BASIS OF RELIGION

BY

SIMON N. PATTEN, Ph.D., LL.D.

PROFESSOR OF POLITICAL ECONOMY, UNIVERSITY
OF PENNSYLVANIA

AUTHOR OF "THE NEW BASIS OF CIVILIZATION," ETC.

New York
THE MACMILLAN COMPANY
1911

All rights reserved

Norwood Press
J. S. Cushing Co. — Berwick & Smith Co.
Norwood, Mass., U.S.A.

PREFACE

I BEGAN writing this book with a simple plan, which was the welding together of the ideas acquired in two earlier fields of work. My "Development of English Thought" was an endeavor to create an economic interpretation of history. This, carried to its legitimate consequences, would afford the objective basis of social progress. I had written also in the field of social psychology. From this a subjective view of these same facts is derived. Religion seemed to me to be the point of union between these isolated views. I thought to use the economic interpretation of history to explain the degenerate tendencies in civilization, and then to employ social psychology to set forth the opposing forces of regeneration. To put this in another way: Degeneration is objective and economic, while regeneration is psychic and personal. This conforms to the views held by religious reformers, and, if correct, gives a firm basis to religious thought. Religion is by this means given a scientific foundation and its doctrines are transferred from the traditional basis to the realm of social science.

PREFACE

On this plan I began to write, and I hope I have not departed from it. There was, however, a break in the process which to some degree modified my plan. After I had written several chapters, a review called my attention to the books of the late much lamented William James. I was influenced by his view of pragmatism, not that it seemed new, but that it was a better expression of a view towards which economists like myself were struggling, but into which they have never clearly come. Professor James, I said, is a philosopher turning towards economics: I am an economist on the road to philosophy; the two seemingly different views should blend and make one truth. Animated by this thought, I wrote several chapters restating pragmatism from a social viewpoint. But in the end I cut out these chapters. I could not enter into a full discussion of pragmatism without turning my book from one on religion into one on philosophy. Tempting as it is to make this transition, the need of clear religious thought seemed too great to permit such a modification of my plan. Now, however, that the book is written, it will help the reader to understand my thought if I contrast it with the well-known views of Professor James. Our likenesses and differences are of such a nature that this can be done without entering into the general discussion that would be necessary if there were not a common basis for our views. Professor James, in a touching way, dedicates his "Pragmatism" to John Stuart Mill. I have frequently taken a similar attitude, and I feel that no honor would be greater than to be one of Mill's disciples. From this common ground both Professor James and I have gone forth. Each has tried to interpret events in the manner and from the premises that Mill would have employed. Two men may, however, have a common master and yet move forward in different directions. How this has happened in the present case can be illustrated by starting with a restatement of Mill's position on the points involved.

To understand Mill demands a study of his "Logic," the place where his views are most fully presented. He there tries to prove universal laws from general inductive experience. This method is the same as that of Professor James who, in his radical empiricism, has the authority of Mill on his side. But a disciple has the right to appeal from this to Mill's subsequent attitude and to the later development of the social sciences. The purpose of the "Logic" was to strengthen social reasoning, and it is by this test that it should be judged. Even while writing the "Logic," a change of opinion came over Mill as to the nature of social proof. This was due to the influence of Comte, by which he was led to put universal historical proofs in the place of those derived from empirical observation. Even this change did not prove satisfactory, for neither in Mill's later writings nor in the oncoming development of social science have either empirical data or crude historical generalizations of the type proposed by Comte served as the basis of progress. Mill made an attempt to write an Ethology on the plan outlined in the "Logic," but was forced to give it up. In its place "Political Economy" appeared, and in this deductive reasoning was freely used. All of his later books follow the logic of his "Political Economy." We are thus left without any evidence that radical empiricism is a fitting method for social science. Nor has Comte fared any better with his historical method. Neither he nor his disciples have given the world anything but crude generalizations, differing in no respect from those obtained by other methods. Doubtless, Mill always held to the hope that universal propositions could be proved in the way he outlined. Professor James is justified in taking up the task and trying to complete the work the master left undone. At the same time, another disciple is equally justified in following the plan that Mill in practice used and which has been the basis of subsequent progress. In no social science are universal propositions accepted on data that would have satisfied Mill and Comte. Particular laws have often been established, but their application is limited to the field from which they are derived. There can be no universal laws unless they are derived from some other source.

The most fruitful law of a general nature is Comte's theory of the stages in the development of thought; but even this must be restated to meet modern conditions. Comte affirmed that thought had three stages, — the theological, the metaphysical and the positive. The concept of stages of thought is valid; but Comte's description of them is defective. The theological stage is really the traditional stage. The metaphysical stage is better described by calling it the critical or skeptical stage, while the positive stage should be renamed the pragmatic stage. Early societies are under the domain of custom, of which religious traditions are a part. Then comes a reaction that takes the form of skepticism, criticism and individualism. This, in turn, is displaced by positive doctrines tested by empirical methods and pragmatic results.

While the validity of these stages is apparent, the order in which Comte placed them is open to question. He used the historical method, and by it the order of the stages is correctly described. The historical epoch, however, does not cover the whole development of the race. The traditional attitude of early races is a result of earlier growth, and of this our knowledge is fragmentary. All traditions must have had a basis in experience and have been proved valid by some facts. The theological or traditional epoch of Comte could not therefore have been the first epoch, and to get at that some other method than Comte's must be used. A better explanation is given by the economic interpretation of history. By it history is divided into epochs, each of which begins with notable economic changes and ends with a social reorganization, bringing a readjustment to the new conditions. In such an epoch the stages of thought development are the reverse of those in general history. The new conditions first affect individuals and are pragmatically tested. Results are formulated as general laws and are then made rules of action. This is the deductive or metaphysical stage. Finally, they become social customs and are enforced as habits. This is the traditional stage to be found in static societies.

If this is a correct statement of the evolution of thought, it has a direct bearing on the way in which universal laws arise and get their validity. New facts are the basis of empirical laws which are tested by their pragmatic results. If the tone of public thought is metaphysical, an endeavor is made to give these new laws a universal validity. A resort is therefore had to

PREFACE

radical empiricism or to *a priori* reasoning to effect this end. Another road is open that does not employ the premises of rationalism in either of these forms. The force of new empirical generalizations is due to the appeal they make to men's interests and desires. The value of general laws lies, not in the greater authority that springs from broad generalization, but in the appeal to new motives for action. The force back of them is the imagination instead of the desires and interests of men. The value of the metaphysical stage of thought arises from its appeal to the imagination that brings action into relation with the future. A double motive for action and a double test of it are thus obtained. Personal or empirical pragmatism is based on present desires and interests. Social pragmatism is based on the future results of acts, and for it to displace the former, the imagination must be aroused and the social motives made active. The metaphysical stage is thus a real advance, even if misused by overzealous rationalists. The subsequent traditional stage also has its advantages, since habitual action is an economy; it is also the only means by which social control can be exercised over ignorant, defective or degenerate men. Each of the three stages thus creates new motives for action, and among them all the truth is made manifest.

PREFACE

If this is a correct description of forces back of the progress of thought, the radical empiricism of Mill and Comte and of James does not offer an adequate explanation of thought processes. Universal propositions and skeptical methods appeal to those who are in revolt against the oversocialization of thought prevalent in static societies. They are thus freed from the social control over action which real progress demands; in its place they put their own personal standards or those derived from physical sciences. Feeling and prejudice may for a time give vogue to these substitutes for social motives; but in the end social standards and pragmatic tests must reassert themselves, for they alone can arouse the whole man to action.

The trouble with the radical empiricist, the skeptic or the so-called positivist is that he tries to stay in the first stage of thought development and thus is compelled to make crude empirical generalizations and personal standards the supreme test of truth. Out of this comes, legitimately enough, a pragmatic attitude; but it is, after all, only one kind of pragmatism. There are two tests of thought, the social and the individual. The personal tests are satisfactions which appeal to the desires. The social tests are objective and are measured by the social results of action. Satisfactions must always remain individual. They afford no test of what society gains or loses by any outlined program. These can be determined by the objective effects that each measure produces. There are three such tests of social results: the economic tests are prosperity, peace and coöperation; the physical tests are efficiency, vigor and longevity; the emotional tests are service, public spirit and missionary zeal. In some of these ways, or through a combination of them, every social act can be objectively tested. The test of individual satisfaction misleads except in crude economic situations where social action is ineffective.

There is thus a social pragmatism which should be contrasted with the radical empiricism that Professor James advocates. The difference between the two, and the test of truth that each uses, may be made clear by a statement of the four criteria that social pragmatism sets up and must defend to make its position valid.

First, the tests of truth are objective and social. Psychic tests are defective, because any degenerate tendency in a man makes his personal satisfactions abnormal. Thought is not a test of truth unless it leads to activity. The only valid personal test is whether or not individual action conforms to social standards.

Second, there are no universal laws. Action is

aroused, not, as the rationalist assumes, by the correctness of formal statements of truth, but by a group of motives of which the formal statement of facts and principles is but a subordinate, although an essential, part. The test of truth is action, and this comes only when the whole man is aroused.

Third, skepticism affords no test of truth. It is merely a shifting from social to psychic standards, resulting in the displacement of social law by individual caprice. Skepticism is either a revolt against the arrogance of social tradition or springs from degenerate tendencies in those who are affected by it. In neither case can it be a part of the forward movement of thought. It may help the individual, but is always socially destructive.

Fourth, the psychic test of truth as a relation between an idea and its object is defective. A philosophical pragmatist may, as Professor James says, accept this as a matter of course, but social pragmatists must look elsewhere for their test. Truth is a relation between thought and act, and not between feeling and its external cause. The truth is not merely workable; it makes men work. If it does not do this, the man is either economically dependent or psychically defective. Ideas are not sense perceptions, but are social impressments, due to activity carried on by men in society.

[xiv]

PREFACE

Their relations are not, primarily, to physical atoms about them, but to the social environment from which they are derived. Thought is adjustment socially acquired; activity is adjustment biologically inherited. All tests of truth must be measures of this joint adjustment, not of the relations of individuals to the objective world.

CONTENTS

[xvii]

Sin is Misery; Misery is Poverty;
the Antidote of Poverty is Income

CHAPTER I

INTRODUCTION

I

This book is not an apology for religion, but a constructive defense. It identifies religion, not with morality, but with the social reaction against degeneration and vice. Were all men moral and normal, religion would have less vitality; it grows in power as the pressure of external conditions forces men into degradation and misery. Religion and morality are the reverse sides of a larger scheme of purifying and elevating humanity.

A generation ago the defense of religion was a subject of popular discourse. Thoughtful men wrote books on Christian Evidence that were widely read and made the basis of popular discussion. Many books are still written about religion, but they are mainly occupied with an exposition of its moral doctrines. It is regarded sufficient if it is shown that personal morality is advantageous and beyond the assaults of adverse critics. It seems to be taken for granted that the beliefs of earlier generations have been overthrown and that religion must utilize its waning forces to uphold morality and social stability. The Christian plan of salvation, however, is as important as ever and as capable of defense.

[3]

It has fallen into disrepute, not because it lacks proof, but because its historical setting has been lost through the increase of knowledge and through better methods of investigation. If we make religion social instead of historical, proof can be found for its essential doctrines. I do not mean that all modern thought is in harmony with the Christian scheme of salvation, but that an energetic defense of it has a fair chance of success. This is made clear by a restatement of the plan of salvation so as to emphasize its modern aspects. The following are its essential doctrines expressed in social instead of theological terms:—

1. The doctrine of one supreme God.

2. The doctrine of the fall of man, or of social degeneration.

3. The doctrine of regeneration, or the reincorporation of social outcasts into society, in contrast with the doctrine of elimination.

4. The doctrine of a personal uplift through contact, influence and suggestion, in contrast with the doctrine of evolution through biologic variation.

5. The doctrine of progress through peace and love, in contrast with progress through conflict.

6. The doctrine of the Messiah, or of lofty inspiring leadership, in contrast with the material concept of civilization.

[4]

INTRODUCTION

7. The doctrine of service, in contrast with self-centered aggression.

8. The doctrine of social responsibility, in contrast with individual rights.

9. The doctrine of personal responsibility in contrast with fatalism or external domination.

10. The doctrine that the wages of sin are death.

Each of these doctrines is capable of a vigorous defense, and if stated in social terms the opposition to them does not come from science, but from a mistaken concept of history. Science is a method of proof, not a dogma. Any problem becomes scientific when it is so formulated that evidence may be collected, sifted and directed to a decision. It is true that every proposition about religion is subject to dispute; but it is equally true that none is without many verifying facts and principles.

The real cause of the decline of religious aggressiveness lies in an opposition not so fundamental, but more potent than science presents. Our beliefs are in the main not directly scientific, but cultural. Ideas and modes of thought are adopted not so much on their evidence as through their power to arouse freshness and vigor of action. Science is merely a contributing element whose dogmas resolve themselves into cultural attitudes rather than scientific facts. All well-established beliefs grow or decline in vigor as the cultural emphasis is shifted to or from the basis on which they rest. We must look to these cultural changes for the causes of the decline in faith. Only when the premises of culture are altered, or those of religion changed so as to harmonize with them, can a revival of Christian zeal be anticipated.

The change in culture that has paralyzed religious thought has many phases but few causes. Expressed in terms of history, the Renaissance, with its revival of Greek learning, and the modern emphasis of nature stand out prominently as causes. Interpreted in economic terms, the cause of the change lies in the shifting of civilization from Southern regions subject to famine, disease and war to those of the North, where peace, security and prosperity abound. Stated in either way, the fact develops that religious thought is bound up with the cultural, economic and political experiences and exigencies of the Southern races. It reflects their views and gives them a universal validity to which the evidence gives no warrant. Culture has returned to the primitive attitude of the pagan world; religion has resisted the change. In consequence, the power of culture has dampened the ardor of those who interpret Christianity in harmony with traditional views. Changes in science are needed much less than a re-

vision of the foundations of Christian tradition. A
broader view departing from this conventional attitude
would give religion a basis in economics and psychology.
Religion would thus obtain a general rather than a
local validity, and be freed from the dominance of any
particular situation or mental temperament. If this
transformation can be wrought, there is little to fear
from science; for it, like religion, gets its basis and its
dogmas from the prevailing social atmosphere. The
two will harmonize when they have the same cultural
antecedents and get their inspiration from the same
ideals.

An example of the contrast between cultural and
religious ideas is afforded by the doctrine of the supernatural, so often cited to show that religion and science
are opposed. Religion uses the language of the desert
or of vile material surroundings. Hence nature is
something bad — the bottom below which men cannot
fall. The natural man is a degenerate because he is
the type such conditions evolve. To get away from
nature means to approach God. With such ideas, it
is proper to speak of Him as supernatural. In cultural language, nature is the highest, not the lowest,
category; for its terms have been coined by men in
happy physical surroundings with nature at its best.
To them the natural man is not the sodden brute of

want and disease, but an ideal to be attained under
favorable conditions. "Supernatural" thus becomes
a meaningless term, because nature is the highest state,
and the natural man better than the best of men. It
is this view of nature that clashes with religious
thought. Either culture must give up its use of
"natural," or religion must adapt itself to it by a
change in its terminology. If the cultural usage is
accepted, "supernatural" must be replaced by some
other term expressing the idea but avoiding the confusion of conflicting usage. This does not imply that
religious thought is wrong in the contrasts it deems
vital. The depraved and the divine are as far apart
when other terms are employed as when "natural"
and "supernatural" are used. And in making this
contrast, science is on the side of religion; for culture
in its nature worship shuts its eyes to the bad that
creates depravity in man. We have only to alter
terms to give scientific form to this important religious
concept.

The doctrine of the fall of man is another instance
of the seeming conflict of science and religion that,
rightly understood, proves groundless. In this case
the opposition does not lie in any essential element of
the religious position, but to the way in which it is
stated. The attributing of the fall to the eating of

an apple is absurd. It is equally plain that there has been a moral and physical fall of man when the man of the historical epoch is compared with preceding ages. There may have been no garden of Eden, but there was an earlier epoch when men attained their maximum of vigor and longevity. Our heredity calls for a life of ninety years, some say of one hundred and fifty years. Man, previous to the last century, did not live on the average more than thirty years, and his health and vigor were far below the normal. From what he was to what he became there is a real fall, justifying the religious doctrine, even if the story picturing it is a myth. This view is supported by the increase of disease, war, famine and crime, bringing degradation to men subsequent to the rise of civilization. The aggregation of great populations in the lowland districts, due to the change from pastoral to agricultural life, the spread of disease, the exploitation of rulers, the decline of physical resources, pushed men down to the lowest limits of misery, poverty and vice. It is in these regions and under these conditions that religion takes its rise; its statement of facts is historically correct and its doctrine sound, even if their pictorial setting does not bear investigation.

A further illustration of how religious doctrines have fallen into disrepute because of the way of stating them is to be found in the contrast between the material and the spiritual. To be religious we do not need to deny that we have material elements in our nature, but only that we are not dominated by them. Religious interest is not in our bodies but in our wills; and freedom is a matter of control, not of essence. We can be spiritual, even though we are material. The real contrast with the spiritual is the traditional. It is the dominance of habit and routine that kills the spirit, not any fatal predetermination of our bodily powers. The "law" to which Paul objects is not a part of our heredity, but the social impressment of past ages. The traditional is objective and social in origin; the spiritual is a psychic reaction against it, a yearning for the freedom that social uniformity prevents. The conflict of religion is between social habit and social feeling. The spiritual is the inner self in contrast to the social self. It is a suppressed heredity battling with the routine and habit of an external world. That there is such a conflict and that the inner self, championed by religion, should be victorious, no careful student of human nature would deny. The right is with religion, even if it states its case in a wrong way.

Another difficulty of the present situation is the use of the term "normal" in the sense of the average man

instead of making it designate the man of full development. The average man has many abnormalities, some
permanent, others temporary; and so long as we
think in terms of him, no clear contrast can be made
between normal and abnormal men. This contrast is
of importance not only in religion but likewise in
every branch of social investigation. A second change
of usage is demanded in our concept of mind. A structural concept has prevailed that makes thought a
definite, predetermined product of some mechanism,
material or otherwise, molded by predetermined conditions. The materialist tells us that the mind secretes
thought as the liver secretes bile. The transcenden-
talist is no less positive about the mechanism of the
mind, even if he expresses his thought in general laws
instead of material examples. Both are parts of a
preëvolutionary view that persists because no reconstruction of our general concepts has taken place in
harmony with our increased knowledge.

In contrast to this structural concept should be put
the genetic concept of mind that causes us to judge it
by its products instead of by its structure or antecedents. The mind modifies its content not only as
it grows but also as the external pressure varies from
which its ideas come. There is no mechanism for
producing ideas. The individual gets them from the

society of which he is a part. They are handed on by an objective social process instead of being the result of the mental mechanism which each individual inherits. Thought is immaterial because its ideas are social, not structural, products. This genetic viewpoint which subordinates brain structures to the social process controlling thought opens up the only way to free mental science from the materialism that structural concepts promote. The brain may be ever so material without doing damage so long as thought originates socially and dominates the action of the brain through the reactions, growth and change it evokes. Similar to the change in the concept of mind is the change demanded in our concept of God and the Universe. So long as space concepts dominate, the universe is thought of as a predetermined structure, definite in parts and unified in character, making God a being with functions complementary to those of men. This attitude is easily understood when we recognize that thought is social and that material and spatial concepts were useful at an earlier date than those of time. Our thought processes thus favor structural views of mind, of God and of the universe. We can change from them to genetic views of fundamental relations only with much difficulty, and against them is always the weight of authority, tradition and language.

INTRODUCTION

Religion begins not with a belief in God but with an emotional opposition to removable evils. It is a psychic reaction, not an intellectual conviction, and its one essential element is its program for saving social outcasts. Our social instincts are thus evoked in its favor, and its opposite lies in the selfish tendencies that would force to the wall those not fitted for the struggle demanded for survival. Out of this background all religions have risen; they will continue to evoke human sympathies and generate religious enthusiasm so long as the present rigid conditions of survival remain. Social activity readily assumes a religious form when men recognize that they sink through degeneration and may rise again through regeneration. Degeneration, regeneration and the will are thus religion's first problems, from which all others are derived. When religion emphasizes degeneration as a starting point, its position assumes both a scientific and a pragmatic quality. The subnormal — below us — is to be avoided; the supernormal — above us — is to be striven for. Religion voices our opposition to the one and our aspiration for the other. So long as men hope to be better, and fear to become worse, religion cannot die out. It cures degeneration through the development of character. Degeneration is the worst of evils; the will is the greatest of forces. Only when these two are put in opposition is progress safe and the supernormal attainable.

The discussions that follow may seem disconnected because they bring together several viewpoints that have thus far been isolated. One of the evils of the division of science into minute parts is that the same views may be held by different groups of specialists, and yet through differences in terminology they may be kept distinct and thus, although one in reality, seem to be parts of distinct disciplines. It is hard to break through these artificial barriers and get at the essence of the recent advances of science. Many seem to resent the restatement of ideas in terms other than their own. Some time ago I wrote to a scientist in a field far removed from my own, and congratulated him on a discovery that seemed to me to be of importance in my field as well as his. I received from him a curt reply, saying that he hoped I would not use his thought, because he was sure I would discredit it by using it in a bad way. Doubtless this is an exaggeration of prevailing tendencies, but enough of it exists to keep apart subjects that are closely related. Science defeats its own ends by a narrow specialization that isolates and antagonizes its workers. As a result, the broader aspects of recent progress are not worked out in a way that furthers general changes in thought which legitimately flow from it. Antiquated scientific ideas persist because the viewpoint of workers is still molded by the ideas of an earlier generation. Little endeavor is made to recast them in harmony with the results these same workers have wrought. Scientific tradition, whether in its social or physical aspects, may become as bad as theological tradition, and for much the same reasons. Philosophy also has become a creed with a tradition as narrow as that of the other groups.

Under such conditions the reshaping of general concepts in harmony with newer facts becomes a matter of difficulty. Evidence of these changes cannot be found in any one field of investigation, nor is there any single discovery that would lead to their acceptance. A writer can at best offer only partial proof, and much he uses will be second-hand material, of which other specialists know more than he does. This difficulty is involved in any general change in thought, and must be faced by any one who attempts it. Whether I succeed or not others must judge, but failure does not necessarily mean that my method is wrong. I shall at least outline problems for others to solve.

CHAPTER II

SCIENTIFIC METHOD

II

RELIGIOUS impulses and sentiments are among the oldest of the race, and have existed with all kinds of institutions, civilizations and degrees of culture. There is no race without some form of religion, and nowhere can it be found so separated from other social facts that it can be studied by itself. It is an alloy hard to isolate, because blended with every other part of the social structure. Every activity is to some degree religious, but none is purely so. Put religion by itself and it disappears, or becomes merely a formal institution, with no vitality outside of its routine. To isolate phenomena of this sort demands a special method and much preliminary study, but if the key is once found and the field of religion plainly demarcated, the subsequent stages of research will be rapid and sure.

A study of method must therefore precede even a definition of religion, for definitions are of no avail when the subject matter is never found alone and nothing else is found except in some way compounded with it. To define is to contrast, and what is there to contrast with religion? At first thought one might say the secular and the religious give a contrast, but here only the organized aspects of religion get a definition. The secular can be contrasted with the ecclesiastical but not with the religious, for the secular life of a nation may express the religious tendencies better than the ecclesiastical. Again a contrast is made of science and religion, but there can be a scientific religion as well as an irrational one. To take for granted that religion is irrational is to give away its case. There are many other contrasts, and yet none of them would define religion. Its essential qualities would be as indefinite as before and as incapable of clear analysis. Only a sound method of investigation can clear away these difficulties and furnish the basis for a clear demarcation of religion from other fields.

The method of physical science seems to many the only one that has advanced human knowledge; in addition, however, the method of economics deserves consideration. Economics for the past century has been the representative social science, forced into the foreground because its material has been so abundant. In the old division of the sciences natural philosophy had the field now taken by the various physical sciences, while moral philosophy had the province now occupied by the social sciences. Had many social sciences developed on a par with each other, the methods of these sciences could be obtained by comparison. But the moral philosophers of England, stimulated by the success of Adam Smith, turned themselves into economists and won their victories mainly within its preserves. For a whole century politics, psychology, sociology and morals were merely by-products of economics — the crude generalizations of men whose main interest was in the promotion of economic thought and the impressment of economic standards on public opinion. It is no wonder, therefore, that the victories won were economic and not sociologic, psychologic or moral. The study of the methods of these thinkers is valuable mainly in economics, and the method they used can properly be called the economic method of investigation, even if it should prove to be the best method for all the social sciences. What, then, is the essence of this method, and how does it differ from that of the physical sciences?

The method of investigation in the physical sciences is not so simple that it can be formulated in terms that would provoke no opposition, yet its leading features can be easily described. It is agreed that all knowledge must be founded on the observation of facts, and that all laws must be capable of an empirical verification. Even if there is some intermediate deduction, a student of a physical science must start with facts and end with them. Observation, experiment and verification are thus the main tools of physical sciences, and many would claim that they should be its sole tools. To employ this method effectively, the object under investigation must be isolated from other objects and contrasted with them. This necessity creates the demand for laboratories, since success in investigation demands complete isolation and exact measurement.

In contrast to this process of isolation and detailed study is the economic method dealing with wholes or with a composition of forces that can neither be isolated, nor studied as single units. Society is a living organism. It cannot be put in a laboratory, nor can its various elements be studied apart from the whole. The method of physical science cannot go beyond a mere statement of what is, and if one attempts to follow it in social studies, he must fall back upon crude historical generalizations or upon equally bad ones derived from a comparative study of nations. These difficulties have forced economists to begin with the study of great changes, which, when consummated, produce modifications so prominent that their effects can be observed. The whole society before a given change can be compared with the same society after the change only when the results are conspicuous. The introduction of free trade into England so radically altered industry and commerce that its results could be easily perceived. In the same way the change from an absolute to a constitutional government produces effects that can be readily measured.

A series of prominent events of this kind gives a body to economic doctrine which can be increased so long as important changes produce effects visible enough to constitute a verification. A direct examination of current facts can never prove an economic theory. The verification only comes in a subsequent epoch when the changes in question have worked out their logical consequences. The economic unit is an industrial epoch, all of which cannot at any one time be directly under observation. Society, as it is, must be put in contrast with itself plus or minus some important condition. Minor changes are ignored, and the whole alteration is imputed to the major modification that society is undergoing. It is this ignoring of minor disturbing causes that creates the marked contrast between economic method and that of physical science. Natural science can isolate minor causes and measure them; social science cannot. It must therefore leave out of account events so unimportant that their results cannot be readily determined. Every important cause is assumed to have one effect and each effect is imputed to some single cause. This method works admirably so long as important changes are under consideration. That it often fails must also be admitted, but if it is the only method of advancing social knowledge, the way in which it proceeds is worthy of consideration.

The contrast between natural science and economic methods can be made clearer by saying that the one endeavors to ascertain *qualities*, while the other seeks for *consequences*. Qualities appear when an object is isolated or when accurately tested by a series of experiments and studies. Consequences follow and are clearly seen only in a distant epoch. The qualities of a germ cell may be observed through a microscope, but no one has ever seen a plant evolve out of some other species. Consequences can be measured only by the changes resulting over long epochs; they are never found in a laboratory. If time is involved, the economic is the only method of investigation.

When this method is used in social science, two distinct types of investigation come into prominence. There must first be found the qualities of men and nature, reappearing with such regularity that they may be said to be the common qualities of men and nature. Most of this work was done by the natural theologians before the reorganization of their work as

[24]

economics. The concepts of a normal man and of a beneficent nature were inherited by the economists from their predecessors. All they have done is to bring out more clearly the characteristics of the normal man and the natural laws that work to his advantage. The successful work of the economists has been in another type of investigation, which also has at its basis an assumption of the natural theologians. If man is good and nature perfect, what is the cause of evil? The economist restates this problem by asking what is the cause of misery? Evil may be subjective, and hence sin, or objective, and then it is misery. The economist has simplified the problem by assuming that sin is a consequence of misery. Remove misery, and sin will disappear. It has no independent existence apart from the misery that bad conditions create. It is but a step from this to the thought that misery is the result of poverty, and thus dependent on industrial conditions. Sin, misery and poverty thus become one problem, and their antidote is income. All three can be wiped out by changes in industrial conditions.

I know of no place where the problem of the economist is better stated than by Henry George. Why does poverty persist with progress? If George had not been in a hurry to give his answer, he would have brought out other assumptions that lie in such discussions. If man is good and nature beneficent, poverty is due to specific causes that can be removed. Economics thus becomes a study of the relations of poverty and misery to bad industrial conditions. It is here that the "one cause and one effect" doctrine gets its importance and reveals its truth, which I will illustrate by the doctrine of free trade. The theory of competition that lies in the background assumes the existence of a normal man and of a beneficent nature. English misery must therefore be due to some specific cause not inherent in normal men nor in nature. Protection is such a cause out of harmony with natural and economic law. Its removal will restore England to a natural condition and enable human nature to express itself more fully in industrial activity. All other causes of misery are for the time ignored, and protection viewed as its sole cause. These assumptions may not be accurate, but if enough misery is removed by a change of industrial policy to make the effect in social betterment plainly visible, the change in policy will be justified. And so it is with other economic slogans. Child labor, the use of alcohol, the lack of labor organizations, the growth of rent, exploitation and woman's emancipation — these like many other doctrines, are boldly asserted and defended by the same arguments, and the success of each agitation is measured in the same way. The net elimination of human misery furnishes the verification to which they must submit. The method fails only when measures are adopted out of their order of importance. The greater evils must be attacked first. Small causes produce no effects until their natural antecedents — the great changes — have produced their results, and men are restored more nearly to normal conditions. The fight for the normal is always made by the elimination of abnormalities. They alone can be tested and measured by the changes that historical epochs produce, and hence their study and prevention is the first work of the economist.

The value of this method cannot be properly appreciated until its power to generate faith in progress and energy in action becomes manifest. The first step in a social reform is a clear contrast between existing conditions and those now possible. It must also be recognized that present evils are due not to general but to particular causes. If there is no contrast between the "is" and the "might be," the imagination has no chance to work ; if evils are due to general and not to local conditions, there is no way of altering them. When clear contrasts are made and the local nature of evils becomes manifest, a social program can be formulated that, setting aside local evils, makes the "might be" into a reality. Take, for example, the social program now forming that would eliminate poverty. To make it effective, people must first see how different the world would be if poverty were removed. But to make this picture an effective motive, poverty must be shown to be due to definite causes. The older view did not permit the isolation of the causes of poverty because they were viewed as resulting from defects in human nature or in natural conditions. The doctrine of total depravity made poverty a general condition from which there was only occasional relief. The law of diminishing returns, coupled as it was with the "niggardliness of nature" doctrine of the classical economists, had a like effect. The abolition of poverty can become a social program only when both these viewpoints are displaced and the particular causes of poverty are separated from the general conditions of prosperity. We can conceive of progress without poverty only as we ascribe poverty to some specific cause.

Picture again the change that is coming in the South because of the recognition of the hookworm as one cause of its misery. The older view assumed that the characteristics of the Southern people were due to their climate and physical conditions. People in hot climates, it was said, are lazy, indolent and imprudent. It lies in the nature of things that they should be so, and that only people north of the frost line can be energetic and efficient. Southern misery thus becomes a part of a general situation — a condition without a remedy. All this is changed by the discovery of the hookworm as a cause of laziness, languor and misery. We can now picture what the Southern States would be without hookworms to destroy the vitality of their people. And this vision of greatness creates the motive of power to work out the change. When an "is" can be put in contrast with a "might be," the "ought to be" looms up with sufficient clearness to make the change. To localize evils always generates enough will power to remove them. The method of isolating evils and ignoring their minor causes is justified by the moral awakening it evokes.

To make use of these facts, tendencies and forces is the end of economic method. The first picture is of the normal man possessing all the qualities of the race, and thus a contrast is created with abnormal environments in which degeneration and subnormal tendencies prevail. Then comes the thought of a normal environment that evokes ennobling human characters, and is never the source of degeneration nor of its consequences in vice and crime. The primal cause of degeneration is failing resources or some misuse of them. Sin is misery, misery is poverty, and the antidote of poverty is income. Such is the message of hope delivered by economics and natural theology when their principles are blended in one discipline. This is the metho that should be used in determining what religion is and how it works. No empirical study of religion can get beyond the petty details that confuse and mislead, but which, when once understood, serve as good illustrations of the principles involved. First the essence and then the details is the only method that will make religion a study fit to be compared with other sciences.

CHAPTER III

THE ECONOMIC INTERPRETATION
OF HISTORY

III

THE concept of a normal man and of normal industrial conditions has thrown into the foreground the motives that create progress. The resulting isolation of the abnormal and local from the normal and general generates the enthusiasm that leads to reform. To localize an evil and to show its abnormal character evoke the spiritual unrest that is the forerunner of revolution. Interest evokes progress; enthusiasm demands regeneration. These two primal forces are aroused and intensified by a skillful use of the economic method of investigation. The method however, has its dangers as well as merits. It succeeds when the relative importance of evils can be accurately measured and public attention concentrated on the greatest of them. But when problems are taken out of their natural order, or the enthusiasm of reformers is dissipated by wrong standards of normality or by the emphasis of minor evils before the removal of their logical antecedents, the path of progress may be barred, and should the dissension persist, a downward move-

D   [33]

ment may result. To insure progress, more than a sound method is necessary. Some way must be found to select between proposed alterations and to test the evidence which various advocates present to promote their reforms.

To meet this urgent need is the aim of the economic interpretation of history. To simplify history and to separate its truths from its errors, some type of society must be accepted as normal, and other societies be judged through its standards. The dominance of economic motives and the urgency of economic needs give to economic societies a legitimate claim to be regarded as normal; and if we further assume that modern nations are more advanced than those of the ancient world, there is little room for doubt but that industrial nations should provisionally be accepted as the standard by whose events the abnormalities of other societies must be judged. The only other wide-spread form of society is the military, whose defects and transient nature are so obvious that no one seems willing to adopt it as a standard by which to measure social structures. It is often put forward as an objection to the economic interpretation of history that there are just as strong grounds for a social, an intellectual or a religious interpretation as for an economic interpretation. Such critics fail, however, to perceive the essential difference between an economic interpretation and those contrasted with it. The qualities of mankind are divided into two groups, the natural and the acquired. For many thousand years there has been little or no change in natural characters. As biologic beings we are to-day what our ancestors were when historians began to keep records: all the changes have been within the group of acquired characters which are in the main economic. Religious, social, intellectual and sexual feelings cannot be regarded as the causes of the changes appearing in history if these feelings have not varied in intensity during the historic epoch. It is only their relation to economic events that has altered, and in this way many institutions have arisen that reflect or reënforce the natural feelings. Institutions, however, are acquired phenomena, and their alterations give evidence of changes within the realm of economics to which natural feelings must adjust themselves. Should industrial habits, methods of production and institutions become stable, while new natural characters appeared, or the older ones gained in strength, a period of history would begin in which progress must be interpreted in other than economic terms. The present epoch, with its fixed natural characters and rapid industrial changes, can have but one valid method of interpretation,

[35]

and that is in terms of its acquired characters impressed and modified by the pressure of economic conditions.

A second reason for beginning social investigations with an economic interpretation lies in the exaggerated importance the economic factors acquire in periods of decay and of diminishing productivity. The poorer the resources upon which a nation depends, the greater is the amount of time that its people must give to earning a living, and the less they have for other activities. The economic discipline thus becomes more severe, and its habits being more deeply impressed, determine more fully the history and institutions of such nations. Those whose energies just suffice to earn a living must lead a life capable of an economic interpretation. Even nations with great natural resources are not free from this exaggeration of economic tendencies, for they have been in the regions most subject to invasion and conquest. Where a military caste, by absorbing the surplus, keeps the workers in poverty, they have conditions no better than workers in nations with meager resources. Exploitation exaggerates the force of an economic discipline even more ruthlessly than does a poverty of resources. These forces were still further increased during the historic epoch by the drying up of the region in Western

Asia and Southern Europe, where the early civilizations were located. In this way region after region felt the force of decaying resources, and went down before physical obstacles they could not surmount. The civilization that arose on this basis could not but bear the impress of the economic events which shaped it. There was no passing on of an improved heredity from one nation to its successors. Only the traditions, institutions and acquired characters were transmitted, and these, from the necessities of the case, were mainly industrial. For such a history there can be no other key than an economic interpretation. If any other viewpoint should in the end prevail, it must have its basis in modern times, when industrial stability is once more secured and the pressure of economic conditions made less severe. But even here economic pressure is too evident to be set aside, and other factors in civilization cannot be fully appreciated until economic forces have been isolated and their laws formulated.

The expansion of this last thought gives a third reason why social investigation should begin with an economic interpretation. The pressure of economic events has modified, dwarfed and subordinated the natural characters so that their present manifestations do not at all represent their full vigor. I freely admit that the social, moral and religious traits are fundamental and of earlier origin than those characters to which economists give attention. In principle, Adam Smith was right in investigating sympathy before he wrote a book about self-interest; but in practice every one fails, just as he did, who tries to study social and moral problems before the effects of economic pressure on these natural traits have been ascertained. The natural man has little chance to express himself when held in subjection by the pressure of external conditions. The revolts against environmental control have been too feeble and of too short a duration to show the vitality and power of the social and moral traits suppressed beneath the routine of daily life.

This subordination of natural traits is often approved because it carries with it the weakening of the impulses and passions of the primitive man. Fear, anger, hatred, jealousy and the sex feelings are partially suppressed by the economic pressure making courage, prudence, patience and forethought and moral restraint the leading characters of civilized races. Were these the only effects, we might congratulate ourselves on the change and think of our moral advance as a net gain. But the suppression has extended to all the natural traits, the good as well as the bad. There is a general blurring of the sentiments that unfavorably affects religion, art and poetry. We lose in inspiration more than we gain by the suppression of passion. The drudgery of modern industry may keep men from becoming very bad, but it likewise prevents them from reaching the loftier ends to which the free working of natural motives would lead them. So long as natural instincts are repressed, we cannot measure the force and vitality of religion and art, which depend so fully on what nature did for man in those earlier days before the economic régime forced a life of routine drudgery on the great mass of mankind.

We regard many characters as natural that are acquired, because they appear so regularly in current events, while the underlying natural traits, seen only in distorted forms, are misjudged and underestimated. In this way sympathy is displaced by selfishness, religion sinks into superstition, democracy yields to imperialism, coöperation is displaced by class struggle, competition gives way to monopoly, and liberty to absolute power. In each case acquired views and habits gain a dominance that so subordinates and distorts natural traits as to make them servants to economic needs instead of masters of our lives and activities. Economic interpretation gives the only method that will unravel the tangled skein of social events and permit us to reach the ultimates through whose dominance alone the goal of civilization may be reached.

Important as are these facts, they do not give the real reason for starting social investigations with an economic interpretation. There are two ways of creating an advance : by bringing out more clearly what is the normal, and by removing abnormalities that obscure it. To get at the normal we need an economic interpretation, but we need it even more to isolate the abnormal and to make plain its source and cause. Evil and sin are either the result of defects in human nature, and hence without a remedy, or they are due to external conditions that mar human nature by producing abnormalities. If the latter view is accepted, the word "economic" must be substituted for "external" in describing the conditions that originate evil and sin. While many good things are natural, most bad things are economic. The good is also the outcome of general laws; the bad is the result of local conditions that may be altered. Evils thus have specific causes that may be isolated and removed. They never arise from the general laws of nature nor from the native impulses of men. Neither nature nor man needs to have his laws altered. Nature is beneficent and man is good ; they become malignant forces only under local conditions that prevent the full expression of natural law and keep men from following their better impulses. To remove the temptation to sin means to do away with starvation, poverty, disease, overwork and bad conditions which depress workers and turn virtue into vice. There is no general law either of nature or of man that forces misery and vice on men. They are local and definite in origin, and may be removed one by one through modifying economic conditions or by the use of the surplus which economic conditions create.

So simple is all this that it would be axiomatic if it were not for misunderstandings that have arisen through the injection of a false philosophy, confusing the economic interpretation of history with a materialistic conception of history. Historical materialism has as its opposite historical idealism. The one claims that ideal or spiritual facts have their basis in material events, while the 'opposite doctrine is held by the idealist. In economic interpretation the problem is not of the dominance of spirit or of matter, but whether a first place shall be given to history or to economics. Shall past events be interpreted in the light of present events, or shall present events be judged by similar events in the past? Both idealism and materialism are historical interpretations, and thus stand opposed to the economic method that interprets

[41]

past events in the light of the present. Abnormal societies, the economist holds, should be judged by normal societies; past nations were more abnormal than those of the present; industrial societies are more normal than those of any other kind. The force of an economic interpretation is increased by the assumption that acquired characters are economic and that the history of the race is a record of their evolution and modification. It is still further intensified by the fact that evils creating social abnormalities are economic in origin, local in nature, and have specific, not general, causes. The end of economic interpretation is to separate the normal from the abnormal and to raise the level of society by removing the abnormalities that check progress and prevent clearness in social thought.

Viewed in this way, economic interpretation is not a new method of investigation, but only a new name for one long in use. The economists derived it from their predecessors, the natural theologians, and have developed it into an accurate instrument of research. Its value consists in the emphasis put on studies of normal life as an antecedent to any investigation of the complexities of modern or historical problems. To show its relation to religion, we must put ourselves in the attitude of the natural theologians who sought to separate the good from the bad and to assign the bad to local, temporary causes. Had they had the thought that evils were economic in origin and might be removed by specific changes in the social environment, they would not have been so easily displaced, and their system might have withstood the shock that evolutionary concepts gave it. Their attitude can be readily revived by reasoning based on an economic interpretation of the confusing facts of history. Only thus can the thread of social progress be followed, and the abnormal be so clearly apprehended that it may be opposed and removed.

Just as economic interpretation had a predecessor in natural theology, so it has a contemporary in the pragmatism of to-day. The two views are the same in their essentials, and stand in contrast to the rationalism and skepticism of the preceding epoch. Both make values ultimates, and measure truth by its effects. To judge the past by the present is to judge by consequences and not by causes. Economic interpretation is thus a particular instance of the pragmatic attitude and the best field in which its worth may be tested. The difference seems to lie in the fact that economists have come to this position from an interest in social problems, while the pragmatists are philosophers tending towards the social viewpoint. Both groups of thinkers are thus more or less inconsistent, because they have not wholly cast off the dogmatic attitude impressed by their education. The errors and inconsistencies of predecessors are not so easily cast off that they may be discarded by a single generation. So radical a change as that involved in pragmatism or in a thoroughgoing economic interpretation of history is a slow growth; but as the various movements blend, they will produce changes comparable with any of the great thought movements of the past. The interpretation of history is but an instance of the interpretation of thought. Analysis should begin with history, because its data are more recent and its material more accessible. Thought is older and more socialized, and its origins are less readily interpreted in terms of the living present. No more principles are demanded for its interpretation than are needed for the interpretation of history. The present is the key to both, and out of it all the categories of thought and history arise.

CHAPTER IV

THE SOCIAL INTERPRETATION OF THOUGHT

IV

THE principle of interpretation set forth in the last chapter has brought out the fact that, while the good is general and nature beneficent, evil is local and economic. The evil can therefore be separated from the general good and removed. The economic interpretation of history thus carries us a long way towards our goal but not to it. It settles a number of the initial problems of progress, but leaves untouched many of the more intricate. To get at the whole truth, the same process of interpretation must be applied to thought as to history. The best records of the past are not in documents handed down to us but in the ideas we get from our mental environment. Error is to thought what evil is to the race. The true and the false are merely particular manifestations of the good and the bad. There is no criterion of truth except that it is good, and none of error except that it is bad. The same law applies to error as to evil. It is specific and local in its origin and can be removed by making definite changes. We need, therefore, to interpret the relation of truth and error just as we have done that

[47]

of the good and bad. The chief obstacle lies in the assumption that we have a faculty for the perception of truth just as we have for seeing red or hearing sound. An act of cognition permits of no interpretation. We must take it at its face value. But if truth is a process and not a perception, we must discount this face value by every element of error that enters the process.

Is, then, truth a process or a perception? A ready and apparently conclusive answer to this is given by those who say that ideas are copies of external things, and that their truth is determined by a simple comparison of the mental impression and its external object. False ideas are thus those that have no external cause; true ideas are those that have something external which they resemble. When this primitive standpoint is abandoned, no firm resting place is found until it is recognized that ideas are social products. We do not start with ideas; we get them as we increase our adjustment. Ideas, moreover, come at the end of a period of progress and not at its beginning. We do not get ideas and adjust; we adjust and then get ideas. Adjustment is a social process. If this be true, the ideas that come out of it are also social, and not the product of any one mind.

The history of particular ideas brings out the same

fact. Each social movement begins with vague notions as to how the old adjustments are failing and how some new adjustment is to be reached. Thousands express their dissatisfaction in crude ways, and others vaguely feel there is a goal ahead worth striving for. Out of these struggles and failures comes a clearer perception both of old evils and of new advantages; finally some one, but slightly in advance of his fellows, sees clearly both the goal and the differences between the old and the new. He sums up the change in a few words, and the resulting contrast opens up to the whole society a new adjustment. Every idea that is a part of our mental atmosphere represents the end of a fierce struggle through which the race has passed. Ideas are our most precious heritage, for they guard us from more evils and lead us to more goals than all other devices and powers.

In face of such facts one wonders how a writer like Professor Green can say that every philosopher starts with a " problem " and a " method," the problem to be solved by the method.[1] Locke, to whom this assertion is specifically applied, is said to start with the problem of the origin of ideas and to solve it by looking into his own mind for their origin. Yet nothing is plainer than that both Locke and his contemporaries stumbled

[1] Works of T. A. Green, Vol. I, p. 6.

about for a long time in the maze of a new adjustment. He and others wrote for decades before seeing their problem or the method of its solution. Their evolution was social, and when clearness came, the epoch of which they were a part was at its end. So is it with all writers and with every epoch. Volumes are written by each great thinker before his clear contrasts come; he gets them not on his own initiative, but through the pressure exerted by his fellows, who are moving with him in the process of adjustment. Why is it that every new thought has from two to a dozen fathers, if the process that creates them is not social and the goal ahead is not some new form of adjustment in which the whole society participates? The reply is that we do not, as individuals, see or create ideas; we get them out of the current of life. The truth of an idea is established before it is an idea. Its presence is its best verification.

We get the same results when ideas are treated analytically. In every idea, sensation, passion, memory and imagination are blended because it has been acted upon many times by each of these faculties before it is clearly perceived. It has also been contrasted with other elements in present adjustment and with the cruder ideas in preceding stages of progress. Not only must it be compounded, analyzed and recom-

[50]

pounded, but it must also be capable of communication and transmission. If ideas did not express other people's adjustment as well as one's own; if the next generation could not acquire them by contact, illustration and example, the net adjustment of the race would be too meager to make men intelligent or life desirable. True ideas promote adjustment; false ideas obstruct it. The greater the adjustment, the greater the truth. There are but two measures of adjustment, the normal and the true. The normal expresses in life what the truth expresses in ideas, for the truth is adjustment made conscious by ideas.

These general tests are too vague or difficult to be available. The practical test of truth is the absence of error. There are few who expect to reach new truth by argument. Most men expect to find it in hidden corners and in unexpected ways after an arduous search in which our fellows join and for which they are partly responsible. But when we want to remove error, we all follow the plan of argumentation, and expect cold facts and skillfully stated syllogisms to drive error out as the sun dissipates the mist or as light displaces darkness.

This attitude overlooks the social nature of error and of its need of interpretation. Every error has a history and is a force. We see this plainly in the case of a superstition or a myth. We know that they have value, and that those who have them do not desire to get rid of them. A creed, a cult, a platform or a program of any sort is tenaciously held, and yields to new social alignments only under great pressure. The cause is the same in all these and other similar cases. They are social in origin, formed from an aggregate of separate elements to voice the sentiments and aspirations of a given age, sect or party. To make a creed or platform enough demands are blended into one program so that, when carried out, definite, measurable changes are wrought in society. All parts of the creed are valued for this gross result, although some one or a few of its tenets may have been the sole cause of the advantage. The tariff and the greenbacks after the Civil War acquired a value because of their association in the platform of the Republican party along with the demand for free labor and national unity. These latter demands, sanctifying the errors in tariff and monetary discussions, have created a situation from which we are extricating ourselves with difficulty. Errors of this kind do not disappear before the mere presence of truth. They have a social worth due to their origin and connection that makes them dear to their defenders. They are the surviving part of an earlier social unit, and get their value from some historic source. We impute to this remnant the utility of the earlier whole, and defend it in the name of the antecedent creed or cult whose emaciated part the error is. Errors are thus historic products or the results of abnormal psychology. In either case their origin is definite and their causes removable. The good is general; evil is local and specific. The truth is likewise general, while error has definite causes. The good and the true are measures of adjustment which evil and error prevent. There is but one final test of all of them — the utility or disutility following the adjustment they create or destroy.

Utility, however, is a standard to be taken only when the loss or gain involved needs no interpretation. This simplicity is seldom attained, for in social matters only great changes can be accurately measured. We must, therefore, in most cases resort to deduction and gain simplicity by connecting evils and errors with their causes in abnormal conditions. But deductive arguments can be accepted at their face value no more than can events or satisfactions. They are subject to the same errors and stand the same need of interpretation. This fact is covered up by the logical canons that science uses. We seem to give certainty to conclusions by the logical chain that unites them to premises, when in reality what we give them is value.

[53]

All that passes down the chain from premise to conclusion is the value stored up in the premise. When
the logical chain is complete, the conclusion gets the
value past experience has given to the premise. That
A is B means nothing unless B, by some previous
experience, is a source of satisfaction, and in this case
there passes from B to A a utility equal to its own.
The satisfaction of the consequent is equal to that of the
antecedent. The logical chain is merely a wire over
which more or less satisfaction passes just as more or
less is stored up in the primary reservoir. The wire,
however, is of no consequence if the battery is not
charged.

The real facts come out, however, when arguments
are considered in detail and the effects observed that
follow their acceptance. All primary beliefs are social.
By this I mean all beliefs have a value stored up in
them that may be imparted to anything deduced from
them. Utilities are divided into two classes, inherent
utility and imputed utility. The inherent utility of
an object always goes with it, no matter where placed
or what its relations are. Sugar has an inherent utility
in its sweetness, and bread in its life-giving qualities,
but the utility of sugar in a cake is an imputed utility.
We know what the whole utility of the cake is, but how
much of it is due to sugar, and what to other ingredients,

is a matter not of perception but of judgment. This judged utility is its imputed utility, and only through a judgment can the utility of any part of an enjoyed whole be determined. There are two rules in deciding upon the imputed utility. If the part is essential to the whole, then the utility of the whole is imputed to the part, and the value of the part becomes the same as that of the whole. If, however, the whole has value without the part, or something else may be substituted for the part, the utility of the part is equal to the difference of the utility of the whole with and without the part. This is called the marginal utility, and it is the utility imputed to most objects. Social units do not follow this rule. The part is essential to the whole, and thus each part must have imputed to it the same utility that the whole has. Logical values are social values. Consequences thus get by imputation the value of their antecedents. The social belief that the premise represents gives all the value the conclusion possesses.

Premises thus are predicates about beliefs and not about reality. The social value of the belief is imputed to all its consequences. A belief, in other words, is a value that has been socially tested. A creed is a group of these beliefs blended into an harmonious whole, and back of creeds are tribal rites, dietary laws, moral codes, folk ways and other early and crude ways of measuring social values. Every social predicate must bring with itself consequences so clear and definite that every member of the group can see its utility. It must not only be proved but proved many times over. All minor values not capable of demonstration are imputed utilities made important by their relation to larger social wholes. Early creeds and moral codes are the best examples of the action of this social process, but the additions made to our beliefs in more recent times follow the same law. Every epoch gives birth to new creeds and moral codes which are tested in the same crude way. The new whole is born a social unit, to the parts of which utilities are imputed. The creation of the new precedes the decay of the old, for decay means not skepticism but a new imputation of values. Some of the older units blend with the new social creeds, and thus get a renewal of their vitality, while others, failing of this, lose the utility imputed to them through their connection with earlier creeds. They die a slow death, as the creed or moral code of which they are a part loses its vigor. Yet, in spite of this tendency, imputed values seem to grow as their social backgrounds fade away. The vulnerable points of a creed are naturally first attacked and most bitterly opposed. As a defense its advocates impute more utility to the parts under fire, until, in its final form, many curious distortions appear.

[56]

The weak points are extolled as of prime value, and the essentials are neglected because unopposed. A dying creed thus seems an irrational product of the imagination, and yet if its history is followed, each step towards irrationality is a logical process impelled by the need of imputing utility to vulnerable points. As an illustration, take the growth of the Southern creed about slavery. As the advantages of free labor became more manifest and the opposition to slavery grew, the South gave more importance to slavery. Religion, constitution and economic welfare all became subordinate to it, and its defense became more logical as its basis became weaker. Such a history has been repeated many times, and each case shows the distortions that beliefs undergo as the imputation of utility to its vulnerable points becomes more apparent.

While this decay in creeds is taking place, another process is transforming their valuable parts into forms not subject to loss. Premises or first principles are the common elements of the various social creeds. To them we impute all the utility of the creeds under comparison. Ethics in the same way is the common element of the various moral codes. The Golden Rule and the ethical imperative represent the essence of the various moral codes, and to them we give a value greater than that of the codes, under consideration. This comparative method is at the basis of all predicates that we call universal or absolute, and by it we seem to get away from the social basis on which judgments rest. Yet the process is one of valuation, even if it be disguised. All universals rest on imputed, not on inherent, utility. Truth is merely desocialized values made infinite in amount by the character of the social facts on which it rests. We get at truth through the imputation of value that follows agreements. We fall into error when the principles that made creeds valuable have been transformed into truths. The decaying creed is thus upheld by a wrong imputation of utility until the skeptic faces it squarely and tests its efficiency.

While skepticism is a natural stage in the progress of thought, no mistake is more fraught with evil than to assume that it is the first stage. It is interpretation and not skepticism that clarifies, simplifies and adds to the positive aspects of thought and blends its units into larger, more homogeneous wholes. As skepticism grows, men become pessimistic. As interpretation proceeds, men become optimistic. Which is the simpler and earlier tendency? The principle of interpretation is nothing more than the first canon of logic — the method of agreement — stated in terms of values. If two objects have certain qualities in common, the value is imputed to these common qualities and not to those in which they differ. There is nothing in an interpretation except a judgment about likeness. The clear, the simple and the essential are raised in value by every agreement, while their opposites lose in the same measure. Skepticism is more complex, for it imposes some external standard not based on mere likeness.

The skeptic comes into religion with the preëstablished premise that there is no supernatural. This he does not get from religious evidence, but from some outside discipline from which he draws his premises. This external standard is necessary in every skeptical judgment. A is always judged through B, never through its own evidence. This means that a skeptical conclusion is always a secondary, not a primary, judgment, and is more complex in its character than are judgments based on simple agreements. Judgments of difference or of disutility come later, and have more elements than those of value and agreement. In social affairs we become aware of differences and evils only in epochs of decay. Skepticism and pessimism appear when beliefs and creeds have lost their vigor. This invariable order shows belief to be simpler and earlier, and that interpretation is the first of our logical processes. Growth preceded decay, truth is older than error, affirmation comes before denial, prerequisites come before consequences.

THE SOCIAL BASIS OF RELIGION

In experience we find ideas, beliefs and creeds so fused that they seem but phases of some one process, yet in origin they are distinct, and must be treated genetically to bring out their differences. Ideas are social products individually acquired. They are the acts of society reacting on the individual, while beliefs are the acts of men reacting on society. In spite of the fact that ideas are only found as constituents of beliefs, the ideas preceded the beliefs in society, while beliefs in men precede the social control they exercise in society. Beliefs start in individuals and at first reflect only personal experience. They are local in origin and reflect the activity of some one man before they are elevated into social forces. This man dominates his group or tribe, and hence his belief becomes theirs and is propagated as a social fact. A local environment is thus projected beyond itself and made the background of social thought. A creed is a union of beliefs derived from a local environment and of such importance that its value can be objectively measured. Its local utility leads to its spread and adoption in larger areas, where it either blends with other creeds and rises into social truth, or, losing some of its essential elements, it sinks into error and blocks progress. This upward blending movement forms the social predicates on which all persons act but no one can test. The downward movement of their remnants forms the superstitions, myths and ceremonies that chain men to the past. Beliefs and the creeds formed from them are never static. They are at first local and vital, then good or bad, and finally true or false. Genetically, all beliefs are vital in origin and get their values from this fact. The vital, the good and the true are but phases of one judgment. The transformations of vital values into judgments of morality and truth merely impute value to elements unperceived in the original judgment.

CHAPTER V

THE SOCIAL PROCESS

V

THE preceding analysis of mental powers and social relations has proceeded genetically, beginning with the simpler forms of life and society and ending with the complex. The method has been one of interpretation, and the steps taken have all been positive. When we are close to the origin of thought, all its complexity is reduced to a few elements, all its values are vital and its laws are based on the method of agreement. The contents of mind in this primitive condition are sensations, reactions and values, each of which the simplest mind has some mental mechanism to produce. There is, however, a fourth content, ideas, for which there is no mental mechanism. There is no idea producing faculty. The mind neither sees nor manufactures them; for ideas are social products acquired from the medium in which the thinker exists. They form a subjective environment of individuals so vital to every act that they are valued more highly than the native products of mental activity. Because of his social proclivities, each individual starts life with a super-valuation of the acquired. It is only by the subordi-

F [65]

nation of his natural instincts to his social needs that survival in complex conditions is possible.

When the social is analyzed into its elements, in the later stages of thought development, fundamental relations seem to be between man and nature and not, as before, between man and society. This stage, however, comes in not by the creation of new faculties but by the recognition of new values. There is but one type of judgment; for all values are in origin vital, sinking or rising as new forms of adjustment place men in closer relation to the world about them. Human progress from primitive times to the present has not resulted from the evolution of additional faculties, but from their utilization in new ways. Each stage in this progress has added new types of value without displacing the earlier ones from which they were derived. The evolution of thought and of faculties differs in that thought changes growing out of new vital relations are not due to alterations in psychic powers. Thought changes are environment changes influencing men through the appearance of ideas produced by new adjustments. Thought change is thus a social change, not a structural change within the mind itself. It is genetic in growth not only for the race but for each individual and age. Each epoch and each person recapitulates the thought history of the race; the new always begins with crude vital values which are gradually transformed into those that more fully express our complex civilization. Nothing is lost; all is transformed. Maturity keeps active the values of childhood. They are absent only in abnormality or old age. Thought is abnormal when some stage is omitted, or when the final stage is not reached. The omission or displacement of stages of thought thus affords tests of abnormality by the use of which we can judge abnormal thought as objectively as we can abnormal bodily traits. No one can rightly take his subjective states or social ideas as ultimates until he has tested them through the normal standards of his age and race.

Appearances and contradictions are indeed made by our faculties, but it is to abnormal and not to normal psychology which we must look for their origin. Every defective faculty presents reality in a distorted fashion, with resulting contradictory appearances. But these distortions of the truth are temporary. Abnormal psychology merely reflects the defects of the environment. The normal alone is carried along by our heredity, and it would, if dominant, reflect the real and make an ever present contrast with the defects and absurdities of abnormal life. It is otherwise with the social process by which our ideas are formed. It works through the acquired traits, and superimposes the values of each moment on the next. In the earlier stages of human progress instincts were developed that forced each person to do what his immediate future demanded. With the growth of complex conditions instincts became less effective and covered less fully the field of human activity. Where instinct failed, conscious motives and acquired traits had to be substituted, and they were made effective only as values increased. The social process cares nothing for error unless it impedes action, and hence it seizes every combination, no matter if inherently contradictory, to attain its ends. Our ideas are social, and become individual only through the routine imposed on the young by their elders. Each man is drilled to see the world as his predecessors saw it, so that their values may become his values. Language, habit and social conventions all conspire to give us a heritage that makes appearances seem more important than the fundamental concepts outside the social process. Appearances and error once having been socialized, it is difficult to get rid of them, even if they become injurious. The social perpetuates itself by repetition and imitation. Another principle than that which originally made things social carries them along. Thought becomes social through its value; it continues social through the routine that habit and imitation impose.

THE SOCIAL PROCESS

It is these two forces together — valuation and routine — that make the social process, and both of them are elements in the creation of appearance and the submergence of reality beneath the temporary interests that impose contradiction and inconsistency upon us. It is not in our perceptions but in our thought that these inconsistencies lie. Our faculties have developed to make perception accurate; thought has developed to increase motives. Thought is thus so blended with perception that we seem to have a unity where diversity exists. The error of thought is that it uses past values given by the social process instead of present values attested by our faculties. Each moment is thus dominated by the values of past moments, and present perception is distorted to put its products into a form that conforms to the need of the past reflected in the present by its values. To the real of the present is added the acquired of the past, and the two, when blended, seem to be a product of our faculties. The simplicity is, however, only apparent. There is always an inherent contradiction when the social has been blended with the natural, for thought processes and psychical processes neither work on the same material nor have the same basis.

There is only one way that thought can be brought into harmony with reality, and that is through the method of agreement. No inconsistencies in thought exist so long as it is used; for it has none of the errors arising from the influence of values on thought. To get at reality we must eliminate every element coming from defective faculties or from social values. The acquired gives us a measure of the social; sound psychology enables us to eliminate the abnormal. Contradiction and inconsistency arise from the influence of one or the other of these sources. The purely real thus becomes the truly normal — the residual left over after the social and the abnormal have been eliminated. This is not something beyond experience but the essence of it. The normal is as much a part of the present as the social or abnormal. Cut off all the acquired factors and disregard the psychic abnormalities of depressed conditions, and a simple reality stands revealed that may be tested by the method of agreement and verified by the normal as seen in the present. This is the genetic as contrasted with the structural view of thought, and is a legitimate consequence of the displacement of the mechanical view of the universe by the evolutionary. The genetic has origins and consequences but no *is*, for it is complete not in a single moment but only in a series of events. Change from the structural to the genetic viewpoint, and the present of things and ideas is not their elements but their value. The reality of things is their origin and consequences, for they are all that time changes reveal.

Is thought an act in time or an element in a mechanism? As we answer this question we decide whether the structural or the genetic shall have first place. And from the decision flows a series of consequences that determine our view of life and character. The structural view puts elements in the foreground that can be compounded into wholes. Movement becomes less important than its machinery. The genetic, however, is synthetic, and its reality is revealed in the normal, which expresses for the moment that which extends into the past and will continue into the future. The abnormal is the temporary, the defective, the unreal. The normal is the permanent, the abiding and the good.

A long evolution has developed in man two powers, the appreciation of objects and the appreciation of ends. Each of these has undergone many changes, but the normal man has both of them in a well-developed form. To keep life going is fully as important as to react successfully against external objects, and the mechanisms by which the normal is preserved are as fully developed as are those that acquaint us with external objects. The normal includes all that is carried along from generation to generation by the physical heredity of the social group. Normal men have enough energy to preserve life and to perpetuate the group. The subnormal lack this energy or in some way have a defective heredity. The supernormal have the complete heredity of the normal, but more energy than is demanded for race preservation. This energy is used for ends other than race perpetuation and makes for the group its social values. The aims and ideals of society are thus set by the supernormal and accepted by the subnormal. The imitative instinct, reënforced by social suggestion, is stronger than that of self-preservation. The whole society is thus transformed from a realistic to a telic basis, which disregards the inherited instincts of self-preservation and even the utilitarian calculus that naturally dominates men. The social is the blending of agreements into unity so that they may become the basis of action. Thought development depends on the evolution of these agreements, and through them the social process gains in strength and clearness until it is woven into the very warp of our being. Differences do not blend into unity the way agreements do. Never capable of interpretation, they remain mere limits to activity until the scientific stage of progress is reached. Primitive men act on agreement and stop at the perception of difference. All early motives but fear are aroused by similarities, which invite approach and as-

similation. The blind instinct of fear is the only unsocial force, and it is active enough to keep men out of the
dangers that differences create. So long as fear is dominant, thought processes do not need to recognize differences. The evolution of thought is thus social until the
progress of mankind has gone so far that fear is no longer
a sufficient safeguard against evil. Then the canons
of logic are extended so as to recognize difference, and
science comes into being.

There are thus three stages in progress from the reign
of instinct to that of reason. In the first, both action
and defense are mechanical reactions against the stimuli
of the environment. In the second, action passes beyond the instinctive stage, but defense and protection
remain unchanged. In the third stage fear ceases to
afford protection, and the basis of defense becomes indirect as well as that of action. The second stage is the
social. Defense is still instinctive, and all differences are
opposed or avoided. In this respect little advance is
made beyond the mere animal stage. A sharp, clear
demarcation shuts out everything except what has a
dominant element of likeness. Within the realm of agreements values rule, because here indirect methods displace the direct. The social is the resulting expansion
and evolution of agreements. A vague, hazy opposition
to the unlike keeps the unfamiliar beyond the realm of

investigation. Mankind has not yet passed out of this stage, for slight differences in race, color or speech still arouse instinctive distrust and prevent the awakening of social feelings. If this is still partially true, we can easily imagine the earlier social stage that arbitrarily shut out differences and thus kept reasoning within the realm of agreements. Then the first canon of logic was its sole canon. The only ends were those of action, and the only values were economic. Men measured what they did by its consequences, and instinctively rejected what they did not like. The consciousness of agreement arouses the motive power by which ends are reached and the vitality of the race preserved. Ideas are agreements that reveal the path along which the race can safely reach its ends. They bind together clear perception and effective action, gaining in value as they stand the test of experience.

The social process, however, has gone beyond the realm of testable ideas and established social predicates that no individual can verify, but which, nevertheless, are acted upon by every normal person. The social forces compel men to live beyond themselves and act as though they were supermen, with powers and faculties above their own. Society anticipates evolution, sets standards above the actual and makes predicates that men act on but cannot verify. The progress of the society living up to them or acting on them gives them their validity. Only the complete evolution of the race can test them. In the meantime, we move along the lines that society has found workable and with the confidence that past experience has given to agreements and actions dictated by them. The social predicates are truths, not facts. Through their pressure the superman of to-day becomes the normal man of to-morrow. God, reality, causation, responsibility and immortality are tested elements of the realm towards which the race is pushing, but into which none of us can go. They are the agreements of racial experience raised by social pressure above the discord and imperfection of the world of sense. If sin, error, skepticism and pessimism arise out of local and special differences not yet harmonized with the wholes of which they are parts, agreements that ignore them have a social validity that no empirical evidence can overthrow.

Of these predicates the concept of God is most important and also most liable to misconception. The popular conception starts with some depreciation of men, and thus makes room for a God to fill in the gap between man and perfection. Some larger task is thus assigned to Him of which men are incapable, with the resulting dependence of men on their Creator, Judge or Ruler. A God of tribulation, poverty and disease is a consolation in disaster, and the accompanying philosophy always springs into prominence when nations, races or conditions decay. This functional God, however, is not a social predicate. Socially, God is purpose, not cause; will not function. He shapes ends, not beginnings. He is the eternal purpose that runs through events, and not the force that initiates them. He does not supplement men and society; he does what they do on a larger scale, with a better plan and in more efficient ways. We rise as we accept His will and bring our plans in line with His. The social God is telic, not functional, and is made manifest in the progress of men and not in their failures.

These two concepts are so blended in religious thought that they seem one, and yet they are opposing concepts due to radically different conditions. They arise from the relative emphasis which thinkers give to the concepts of space and time. If the universe is pictured as an object in space, and all its contents are measured in spatial terms, God acquires a different meaning from that He has if the universe is thought of as a process in time. Matter and energy each represent a view of the universe, the one in terms of space and the other in terms of time. The mental process, however, by which we attain these two views of the universe is the same. Ask for foundations; separate them from the superstructure, and the spatial view of reality is acquired. Ask for continuity and activity; view as temporary everything that does not continuously manifest itself, and we exclude from the ultimates of the universe all temporary conjunctions and dead relations. What is it, however, that has continuity and activity but no permanent spatial form? We must ask this question to get a clear contrast between space and time realities, and we must acquire habits of thought that make continuity and activity persistent before the crust of habit will be broken, favoring a spatial view of the universe.

Philosophy, following the lead of the earlier physical sciences, has committed itself thoroughly to the spacial view. The social sciences have at least partially freed themselves from its control, and it is in them that a better development of time concepts has taken place. This has been due to the need of using history and to the fact that the units making a society are not permanent. The units representing the normal type are constantly changing, and yet the type persists and gives to nations their unity and history. The normal is thus a time concept as important in its field as is the corresponding concept of matter in the realm of space. Shut out all the incidental qualities of material things, and the concept of atoms arises. Shut out the temporary qualities of men, and the normal is the enduring residual. The abnormal is always prominent and apparently dominant, yet it is only a temporary phase which is constantly reappearing but never enduring. Back of it are the normal processes which hold humanity to its standards and from which alone the trend of progress is ascertainable. The real is that which may be incorporated into the normal. All that is normal is real. All that is real may be made normal. It is not the oneness of things but the oneness of type that gives unity to the universe.

To show that time concepts are fundamental, and not an offspring of those of space, needs a thorough realization of the fact that all ideas are social and the result of a process instead of being immediately given or psychologically made. To socialize an act through habit and imitation and to conceptualize an element in consciousness are different phases of one process. We cannot form and retain a concept except as it is passed over to others, and its usefulness is tested in their experience as well as ours. The concepts a man uses are not the full reality of his experience, but only that part of it which has been socialized. Conceptualized time is the part of time reality that has been socialized, and for like reasons conceptualized space are those elements in space reality that have become socially useful, and hence constantly revived and passed on by social habit. Concepts in neither case are taken directly from reality by perception, but are imposed on individuals by the social process antecedent to experience. They are never all of reality. There is always a residual in reality which concepts never reveal.

Concepts are a heritage, not an individual creation. They always fall short of the real because they represent the socially useful, and are never modified or enlarged except as new aspects of nature become important to men. Beyond them is always a residual that is constantly encroached upon by the growth of thought, but is never exhausted. The normal represents the parts of the social process that are complete; the residual is the beyond, always directing men's efforts, but never being completely absorbed in the normal. The supernormal includes elements of the residual plainly in sight but not yet embodied into normal life. By it the normal is elevated, and the social is extended into new fields. The link between the unincorporated residual and the normal is thus the supernormal, and to it all the telic processes are due. The normal must move towards the supernormal, which is made real by the elements of the residual capable of being incorporated into the normal.

It is a practical reversal of our religious education to associate God with the residual instead of the primary forces of nature; and yet this is what we are compelled to do if we shift over from a view of the universe that makes space concepts fundamental to one that gives a first place to those of time. Space reality demands a basis on which the shifting, unstable sensual appearances can rest. God thus becomes that from which all else springs and through which it obtains its unity. This concept of God is made real by the feeling of depravity so firmly associated with religious life. We feel that there is something in us that leads to destruction unless our weaknesses are supplemented by a power higher and stronger than ourselves. To think of God as a residual force demands that we put the normal in the foreground, instead of missing functions and depravity. Both these concepts presuppose the normal, and would be meaningless without it; and yet the ordinary person has had depravity so thoroughly impressed on him by the imperfections of life that he thinks of humanity as being in a subnormal condition, and thus without hope except by the intervention of the supernatural. The corresponding concepts in time reality are parts of experience. The subnormal, the normal, the supernormal and the residual are all within experience and are separated by no absolute lines. The normal can sink into the subnormal or rise into the super-normal, and the residual, although indefinite and un-measurable, is always in sight and is incorporated into the normal by every progressive social change. God and man are not distinct in kind, but as man incorporates the godlike into himself by his social progress, newer views of the residual that lie between himself and per-fection make God appear to be even more different from himself than He formerly seemed to be. God is a being on whose trail we always are, but whom we never can overtake. We approach Him only to find ourselves farther off than before.

CHAPTER VI

THE STAGES OF THOUGHT DEVELOPMENT

VI

Of the various attempts to coördinate the sciences, that of Comte is the best known. Each member in his series is more special than the one before it, and depends upon the facts of all the sciences preceding it. The first and most general of the sciences is thus astronomy, while the last in order, and most concrete, is sociology. Between them come physics, chemistry and biology in the order named, with a possible place for psychology, when this subject gets its facts well enough coördinated to show its worth. Back of this scheme, however, and serving as its basis, is Comte's doctrine of stages in human thought. In the early epochs of history men are theological; then they become metaphysical, and finally positive in their thinking. The theologian disappears before the philosopher, and he in turn gives way to the man of science. The scientist does not start in a virgin field, but begins his work after myth, superstition, creed and dogma have been formed by the theologian and further distorted by the metaphysician.

If Comte's conclusions are to be doubted, the real

issue is not to be taken with the sequence of the sciences, but with the preliminary work by which the field is cleared for scientific investigation. If it is asked how did the philosophers displace the theologians? the reply must be, "Mainly through their skepticism and pessimism." It is true that the philosophers had dogmas, but they laid the foundation for their principles through skepticism and not through positive research. Comte overthrows metaphysics by using the skepticism philosophers devised to discredit the theologians, and thus clears the field for the positive methods of the sciences. In this way skepticism lies at the basis of Comte's system. If the philosophers were wrong in using it to discredit theology, Comte is in the wrong when he employs it to clear the field for positivism.

What, then, is the basis of skepticism? Here is the fundamental problem on which all else turns. Skepticism cannot be made the logical starting point of science if it presupposes the very things that science must establish. To be skeptical we set up objective standards so that the object under criticism is judged by something different from, and superior to, itself. Skeptical conclusions thus depend on the truth of the second logical canon, the method of difference. And this method can seldom be used except where experimentation is possible. It presupposes the uniformity of nature, and thus cannot be used to prove the very law its premises assert. To doubt involves an affirmation, and no doubt is effective unless it assumes some antecedent objective truth. Theology and metaphysics must have left something positive, or science would have been unable to start on its most useful mission.

In contrast to the method of skepticism is that of interpretation. If skepticism fails to give a starting point, it is worth while to test what interpretation can do. It depends on the principle of identity and similarity, or, in other words, on the first canon of logic. The method of agreement is based on observation, and decides which of two similars is simpler, clearer or more valuable. The method is always positive, never negative. There is a comparison of A with B, and the conclusion is merely that A and B are identical, or that B is not like A, and hence has none of its qualities or value. Two like objects have the same value, but if they are unlike, the inherent value of the whole lies in only one of them. The other, a nonessential, is thrown aside as spurious. Interpretation thus simplifies and brings to the fore the great objects of human interest. Its method is always positive. It adds to social values, enunciates principles, and gives simplicity to whatever it is applied. The evolution of thought it promotes retains the essence of each stage to form the basis of the next. The crude beliefs of the primitive world are refined and elevated, until they finally appear so different from what they were that they seem new creations. They are, however, the same beliefs in a new guise, for the evolution of thought has been positive except where it has been disturbed by skepticism. Had philosophers used positive methods, this view would have been clearly established long ago; but in their haste to overthrow theology they used the cruder and faster working tools of skepticism, with the result that they fashioned weapons which discredited their own work and forced science into an illogical position.

Physical science deals in uniformities; social science deals in values. Which is the older viewpoint, and which helps us most in understanding the evolution of thought? It is so generally admitted that the first stage of thought is theological that we will hardly do wrong to begin our investigation there. Folklore, myths, superstitions and creeds are so plainly matters of belief that the verification they found in the primitive mind must have been based on their usefulness. All original values are handed down from generation to generation as beliefs formulated in creeds and moral codes. The acquisition of the useful thing creates a social habit which in turn crystallizes into social law. As old usages sink into superstition, new ones more suited to progress spring up to support the social fabric. Values grow in every society and form the test of progress. The metaphysician tries to get a basis for these values by attaching them to something beyond. This would have been a useful process if he had not combined it with skepticism in a crude and forceful attempt to destroy primitive beliefs. The result, however, was confusion and the need of a new start; for skepticism utilized its advantages so skillfully that it discredited first principles of philosophy as fully as it did old religious beliefs.

The new start lacks a good name because the two names often applied to it have associations that mislead. To call it utilitarian is to associate it with a narrow type of morality; and to call it economic brings to mind modern business problems instead of those of the primitive world. In a broad sense economy is the relation of effort to return, and in the economic world beliefs, like goods, rise in value as they increase the surplus of reward above effort. At the basis of every economy are two laws: the law of parsimony and of the uniformity of nature. We now attribute the uniformity of nature to science, and this is true if we think only of the modern extensions of the law that have given it universal validity. But the earlier examples of the law were found in agriculture, commerce and industry. The return of the seasons, the growth of crops and the propagation of plants and animals taught men the uniformity of nature long before laboratories were thought of. All these uniformities were capable of direct observation, and were useful in pushing men over from a nomad state to agriculture and commerce. The nomad could truly be called a theologian and a metaphysician, while the agriculturist was a utilitarian and an economist.

Comte was wrong in saying that the positive stage of thought follows the metaphysical. Had he lived in our day, he probably would have made the pragmatic the third stage instead of the positive. The contrast between the metaphysical and pragmatic is clearer and more important. The metaphysical judges through causes and antecedents. The pragmatic, through consequences. This change in thought clearly marks one of its epochs. In social science economic interpretation is also a judgment through consequences, and therefore a part of the same thought epoch. The real contrast is with the historical method, judging the present through its antecedents. Comte's method is historical, and thus he falls into the errors natural to rationalism. It may be a question what he would do if he had our knowledge and mental attitude. There can be no doubt but that we should divide the development of thought into different stages from what he did and make the order of its development social instead of rational.

There is also in his plan a mixture of two thought movements, the one that the race follows in its uplift, and the other that the individual follows in his growth. The stages in race progress are all positive, and follow changes in the social attitude. In this way we get the theological, the metaphysical and the pragmatic. The individual, however, begins in an epoch of faith, after which comes an epoch of depression and skepticism, and this in turn is followed by an epoch of idealistic realization. Depression and skepticism are an almost universal stage in the forward movement of individual thought, but he who outgrows it may pass on to an idealism that gives a vision of remarkable clearness and power. The social, however, has stages neither of skepticism nor of idealism. They reflect merely a personal movement of thought, which becomes a source of confusion when attempts are made to give it a social basis. Individuals tend to become idealistic, but the societies of which they are a part move steadily towards the pragmatic goal. The forward movement of thought is thus from theology through metaphysics to pragmatism. The epoch of science comes much later, and is not so much a new epoch as a wider extension and a fuller appreciation of the uniformity of nature.

THE SOCIAL BASIS OF RELIGION

The oldest and best-established uniformity is that between effort and reward. When this is perceived, men begin to judge acts by their consequences, and social values arise, displacing the primitive beliefs which recognize no causal relation. The will of man may be or may not be itself caused, but the consequences of acts can be definitely foreseen and measured. The first predictions thus relate to happiness and misery and create the social values we call utilitarian. This early economic stage of thought, with its empirical standards, did not abide. Men pressed on to a higher level not by displacing empiricism but by transforming its cruder values into higher forms. Logic is a device to test values. It gives to each part of an economic whole the value that makes its continuance or reproduction possible. The law of parsimony is but a general statement of the economic law of the greatest gain for the least effort. Keep economics concrete and logic abstract, and the two seem to depend on separate mental processes and predicate the existence of distinct faculties. If, however, the logical process does not affirm reality, and the law of causation is a social, not an objective fact, it has nothing to distinguish it from the process of valuation the economists use when they compare the utilities which various articles possess. Value measures effort through product, cause through consequence and the object through the feelings it evokes. Logical values impute to the part the value of the whole. The laws of logic are thus the laws of imputing utility, the same laws that the economist uses to measure utility in any complex act of production or consumption. To judge by consequences is the utilitarian or moral stage of progress; to judge consequences by their antecedents is the economic or logical stage. The one gives prominence to the empirical measures of value, while the other uses deductive tests. The end of logic is thus to test the imputation of value following the use of social predicates. The belief in the whole implies a belief in the parts. Every right imputation increases efficiency, while every wrong imputation creates misery and maladjustments. Logic thus prevents waste, and is the first form of the conservation of energy. We must recognize and conserve human energy before we can that of the universe.

Much of the confusion about the relation of logic to social facts arises from the overemphasis of space concepts. Sensations and material objects relate to space, and they create contrasts more definite and more easily seen than those of time. The result is that they have received greater attention, and when men begin to doubt they start with denying time relations. The ultimates of the universe are thus shifted over into space, and reality is defined in its terms. Exclude the genetic from thought, and a static universe is manifest. Exclude, however, all space relations, and the resulting categories give a view of the universe that cannot be so readily unified, and if pictured, it must be not as a mechanism but as a movement. All mechanisms are spacial; time is a process, not a completed whole.

It is easy to understand the subordination of time to space which has taken place in philosophy when we realize how it has been helped on by the growth of language. The older substantives are spatial concepts because the interests of the primitive man are material. Things are his reals, for on them his welfare depends. He thinks of time through the modifications it makes in things, and hence the words he uses to describe change are adjectives. When conscious materialism begins in a later epoch, this state of the language favors the contention that the essence of things is material. All primary qualities are now said to be spatial. Only the extended is real. In this way time relations appear to be secondary qualities having no place among the ultimates of the universe. This advantage in suggestive power has been largely lost by the later developments of language due to the increase of scientific knowledge. Many time concepts have a substantive form of expression, so that we may think in terms of time almost as readily as in those of space. We can excuse Hume, Kant and others of their age for their over-emphasis of space, but the same emphasis to-day is due merely to habit, continuing modes of thought that should be modified or displaced. With our improved language it is no more difficult to think in terms of energy than of matter, and we can picture the world as a process quite as readily as an abstract "thing in itself." For the purpose of contrast I shall place our leading space and time concepts in parallel columns. This will help the reader to judge which are to him the clearer and more fundamental.

Matter	Energy
Form	Motion
Position	Activity
Perfection	Evolution
The infinite	The normal
The real	The valuable
The omniscient	The supernormal
Structure	Function
Static	Dynamic
Force	Will
A thing in itself	A process
The absolute	The genetic
God as creator	God as purpose
Materialism	Idealism

The spatial terms need no explanation, but it may be worth while to bring out more fully the time element in some of the words in the other column. The normal is the present of that which has had a past and will have a future. It is thus a time concept, even if it perpetually renews itself in material forms. The supplement to the normal is the supernormal, but the line between the two must not be drawn in the same way as between the corresponding space concepts. The supernatural implies being completely outside of nature, and the superhuman is divorced from organic life, but the supernormal is natural and in some of its expressions it may be human. The best of men continually reach out beyond the normal and incorporate in themselves some of the supernormal. The normal is constantly rising and making the supernormal a part of itself. The supernormal thus loses on one hand through the growth of the normal, and gains on the other through a clearer concept of the process by which the universe unfolds itself. It is not an independent whole, but a residual always losing to the normal, but never disappearing. This residual element separates time concepts from those of space. Evolution is always going on, but never complete. Processes find new energy to continue them. Unity and perfection are spatial. Time is full of residuals that block their attainment.

THE STAGES OF THOUGHT DEVELOPMENT

The stages of thought thus far enumerated are due to positive evolution based on interpretation and the use of the canon of agreement; the age of faith is thus transformed into the age of dogmatic assertion; this is displaced by the moral stage, where acts are measured by their consequences; and then comes the age of logical valuation and economic deduction, which tests the imputation of social values and brings out clearly the relation of effort to result, cause and consequence, will and achievement. Social values are thus dissolved into their elements, while their clear ideas and ultimate predicates are measured by their intrinsic, and not by their imputed worth. When this is done, the basis for the age of experimentation is laid and the second canon of logic, the method of difference, can be used to test everything not bound up in social predicates. Social units never can be tested experimentally because the parts cannot be isolated from their wholes.

Society is a process, not an objective fact open to observation. The past and the present are so intimately related that the one cannot be understood without a knowledge of the other. The traditions, habits and modes of thought coming from the past have not remained unchanged, so that they give us a correct account of past events. What we call the past is not the pure past in the way that atoms and extension are pure space. The past is made by the present, or at least so reshaped that its purity as a past event is lost. What we know of the past is altered by every new force that makes the present. What made yesterday also makes to-day. If we understand these forces, and get a clear view of the normal connecting the past with the present and running through both of them, the main elements for the interpretation of past records are at hand. The true past has left no record. The social process carries along nothing but what is of use in the present, and that it remodels to meet present needs. The valueless drops out of memory, is lost sight of by the historian and is eliminated by the thought processes that are centered on the present. We must know the present to know the past, for only through its laws and pressure can we discover the way the past has been altered to meet our needs. These facts give validity to the economic interpretation of history and make it necessary to begin a study of social science within the realm of economics. The moving values of to-day are economic, and through them is the best entrance to the study of the forces shaping the present and thus determining normal life.

So much for the general principle. Time forces must be studied in the present and not in their records. The present of the past is its values, which remain the one sure test of how past activities react in the present. Records, traditions, words and thought only tell us how the past appears in the present, but not its real essence. The constantly repeated is the true, and this is the normal. Conditions make values, values make motives, motives shape character and character is the index of normality. All the real is thus in the present and can be observed at first hand. We can only unfold the present by starting with conditions and ending with a study of the normal life that matches them. Conditions, and not antecedents, are the source from which the social sciences arise. Antecedents are thought, not reality, and have in them the errors that our thought processes create or absorb from the social medium in which they arise.

The beginnings of social science thus being in present conditions, economics is the first social science and the basis on which all the others rest. To go out from the present practically means to go out from economics, for it is the science of normal life and its values. If all time antecedents are appearances, the data of to-day's life must be studied to get the key by which past records and memories can be understood. There is another view, however, which gives the same results without so much abstract thinking. The traits of men are either natural or acquired. Conditions act on men through their acquired characters. The routine of life is impressed on individuals from without with such force that the natural characters are suppressed. We cannot begin with a study of natural characters, because they are revealed to us only in such mixtures with acquired traits that our observations have little value unless we have first measured the extent and activity of the acquired characters. Most of the social, as well as the economic, forces lie within the realm of acquired characters and give them their dominance. What we think to be natural is mainly acquired. Tradition and economic routine mold our lives so early and firmly that we accept their impressments as a part of ourselves. The acquired characters must therefore be studied first, and then the social process by which the acquired traits are impressed. Only when these two are thoroughly understood can natural characters be investigated to advantage. They are a residual which in real life becomes isolated enough to make scientific study possible only as a remnant for which the laws of acquired traits can give no explanation.

The peculiarities of religion are due to these facts. It is not an instinct nor any single motive, but a complex due to the pressure of external conditions on deep-seated race traits. The external conditions are mainly economic; the internal reactions they arouse make

[100]

social psychology. The form of religion in any age is due to the interaction of these forces, and it has developed as men have become more conscious of the inherent opposition between the pressure that creates routine and the freedom which permits a full expression of inherited traits. This opposition takes on a social form when it becomes manifest that external pressure lowers vitality and eliminates the weak. To sink to a lower level of vitality is degeneration. To reincorporate the weak into society demands their regeneration. Degeneration and regeneration are thus complementary themes, and from their union comes the plan of salvation that is the center of religious thought.

Religion is thus a natural movement based on social feeling, and focused by external conditions. It is an expression of a reaction against conflict, degeneration and depravity. God's activity is the complement of men's endeavors to restore the normal and to elevate social standards. When men's depravity and helplessness were appreciated in primitive times, a God of infinite power and knowledge became a necessary part of religious thought.

It is a reversal of the order in which religious ideas developed to make religion begin with God, instead of basing it on the natural phenomena out of which it has arisen. The problem of God will lose its difficulties, if men once become familiar with the laws making them fear degeneration and hope for regeneration. The key to religion lies in these problems. Having explained the economic pressure creating degeneration, we must next treat of the psychic problems that arise because of its prevalence. The seemingly sudden change from the discussion of external pressure to internal psychic reactions is justified by the really close relation that exists between the two. The social psychology of religion is either a group of acquired traits due to external pressure or a natural reaction against it. Neither element can be studied except in close connection with the objective conditions that create them and arouse their activity. First the economics of religion and then its psychology.

When, however, the proper preliminary studies have been made and the laws of the present have been thoroughly investigated, a field of fruitful inquiry is opened up to which neither economics nor a knowledge of the social process gives the key. The routine of life imposed by external conditions suppresses the natural characters and makes them more difficult of study. Only the strong emotions arouse them and make them dominant. It is in the field of passion we see the power of the natural traits and have them vigorous enough in their manifestations to render their study profitable. The discipline that deals with passion and emotion is religion, and for this reason its study becomes the second in order of the social sciences. Economics emphasizes objective conditions and mental routine. Against these, religion is a revolt. Through its emphasis of passion and emotion, it brings into prominence the residual in human nature that economics neglects. We call natural traits depravity when their activity should be suppressed. We call them inspiration when they should be followed. As we become religious, the natural characters are evoked; as we become economic, they are submerged beneath a life of routine. The two disciplines thus supplement each other and between them the elementary facts of social science are brought into the light. There is no other entrance to social science so fruitful of results as that which puts into separate fields the study of natural and acquired characters. There has always been a crude tendency to make this division even before the basis on which it rests was clearly seen. Now, however, it is possible clearly to demark the two fields, and to give to each its appropriate place.

CHAPTER VII

MORBID DEGENERATION

VII

THE discussion of degeneration has passed through so many phases that a lack of definiteness has arisen in the use of the word. Various problems have been brought together which must be handled separately before clearness of thought can be attained. The primary confusion is due to a lack of differentiation between cases where individuals fall below the possibilities of their heredity and those where two types with somewhat different heredity are mingled in one society. We call thieves and prostitutes degenerate because they lack normal traits. Yet they may have developed their heredity as fully as have the people with whom they are compared. They may be survivals of an earlier condition in which so-called degenerate qualities may have been normal attributes. It is better to call these persons static than degenerate. It will then appear that the normal individual is a product of evolution, and not that his social inferior comes into being through a degeneration in type.

The prevailing terminology is an outgrowth of the old concept that men began in a perfect state and hence that present deficiencies are degenerations. It will take time to get rid of this primitive concept, and so long as it persists the prevailing social use of the term will obstruct clearness of thought. There is a concept of heredity that also helps to keep alive this view of degeneration. It is often asserted that all differences in individuals are due to differences in the germ cell with which development begins. For each character manifested at maturity there is said to be a determinant in the germ cell to which its appearance is due. Heredity builds true; hence diversity in results shows antecedent differences. Degeneration thus comes to mean a lack of some of the germinal elements that appear in normal persons. There can be no doubt that degeneration of this type takes place. A comparative study of animals shows that it is going on all the time. Still, it may be doubted if this sort of change is at the bottom of the prominent differences manifest in human beings. It is a process that accounts for changes in type rather than for those found within a given type. If each type has a normal standard about which it varies, the deviations from it in one way or the other must have some other cause than that which produces new types through natural selection. We might, without much abridgment in the use of popular terms, call those germinal differences that result in a lower type of organization abnormalities. We may then contrast with them maldevelopments which indicate the wrong direction in which growth processes have been forced. In such a contrast, abnormalities would be due to difference in heredity; maldevelopments to external agencies. Abnormalities are also negative, since the abnormal person lacks in his heredity some determinant that normal people have. Maldevelopments, on the contrary, are positive and represent a growth — a change from the normal type due to a turning of vital forces in a wrong direction. In a maldevelopment, the energy that should go out in the normal direction at a given time goes out in some other direction or at a premature or overdue period. Maldevelopment is thus a problem of energy and not of heredity. If this contrast becomes clear, the two ways in which deviations from the normal take place can be readily understood.

Another way of illustrating this difference is to make a contrast between the germinal forces, that develop into the mechanism by which life processes are carried on, and the nutritive forces, that give the organism its efficiency. The mechanism of life comes from the germ cell. To this nothing can be added by the growth of the organism. Nutrition comes from without. It is constantly absorbed and given off.

Hence its presence or absence at critical stages of development does much to determine the direction or lack of direction in the subsequent growth of the organism. It is an error to regard a germ cell as having within it but one group of possibilities. It is more in accord with the facts to say that development from the germ cell proceeds in a certain general direction within limits that vary as the external conditions promote or retard its progress. Heredity is a reality, but it is not so definite nor so mechanical as is generally supposed. Nutrition is responsible for much that passes for heredity. Only after its effects have been definitely ascertained can the real mechanism of heredity be understood. Why, for example, does each organism reach maturity and finally sink into old age? Is there a determinant in the germ cell that when active checks growth? Does the mechanism of life run progressively to a certain point and then refuse to act? Or is maturity merely a state of maximum nutrition and old age a running down because nutrition fails? To state the problem in another way, Does a given organ cease to grow because the possibilities of its inherited mechanism have become exhausted, or does growth end because nutrition fails when the energy of the organism is turned in other directions? The latter is, I believe, the sounder view. Each organ grows while nutrition comes its way; it stops growing when a more favored part absorbs the energy that hitherto made its growth possible.

There is no mechanism that stops growth except by turning the flow of energy in some other direction. The organs or parts develop in turn, each checking the growth of its predecessors by absorbing the energy they have previously had. If new organs appear at the right time, the growth of the whole organism is normal. If the new organs appear sooner or later than normal, maldevelopments arise. In such cases, the flow of nutrition to the older parts is either extended beyond the normal time or taken from them before they have attained their normal growth. Maldevelopments are thus nutritive in origin and arise whenever the ordinary sequences of development are disturbed. If the growth of an organism is accelerated, — that is, if new parts appear before the older ones have attained their normal development, — the latter are prematurely checked, and the organism is maldeveloped. So also if the newer parts are slow in development, their predecessors keeping the extra nutrition longer than usual, the former grow in unusual ways. Retardations and accelerations in growth thus cause organisms to deviate from the normal. Heredity has no way of keeping growth along normal paths except by starting new organs at the right time. Older parts will grow until nutrition is taken from them. They cannot reach the normal standard if a premature change in the flow of energy takes from them the basis of growth. Normality is thus a problem of nutrition and not of heredity. Acceleration and retardation in growth are the cause of maldevelopments.

This thought merits further expansion, because if true it leads to important results. Growth has two conditioning factors: (1) the constitution of the germ cell with its effect on subsequent development; and (2) nutrition, which coming from without may create states of surplus or of deficit. A surplus of energy causes parts to grow longer or in a different way than they would if the surplus were less or if it had been turned in other directions. These overgrowths are malformations, judged by normal standards. They are natural growths, however, and are injurious because they use up energy which could be more usefully expended in creating newer parts. If older organs have too vigorous a growth, the newer ones are but partially developed or are less active than the older. The organism thus assumes a type similar to that produced by a lower or defective heredity. It shows atavistic traits, not because of a defective germ cell, but because of an overgrowth of its lower organs.

[112]

A shift in the relative growth of parts reveals at maturity the same characteristics that come from a defective heredity. The balance of an organism once disturbed, subsequent development never rights itself. It continues along abnormal lines just as if this direction had been given it by an original impetus coming from the germ cell. Defective heredity and mal-developments thus give the same results and have the same marks. They lower the general tone of the organism, submerge its higher traits and make prominent the characters of its primitive ancestors. Retardations are thus overgrowth of the older parts that check the upward movements of an organism. There seems to be a lack of the higher faculties or only a partial development of them. This, be it remembered, is due not to any failure in heredity, but to the dwarfing influence of an overgrowth of the older parts. The drop in the scale of existence is not a permanent one; for if the overflow of energy to lower organs is stopped, normal development is resumed. In any case, the next generation will not be affected unless the external conditions causing overgrowth are repeated. Acquired characters have no vigor apart from the conditions that produce them.

In contrast with retardations due to overgrowth, accelerations cause energy to flow too rapidly from

lower to higher parts. The lower parts are dwarfed
instead of the higher. An earlier maturity results
with all the vital organs more or less deficient in their
development. Each organ falls short of its full development in ways that can plainly be observed. Yet we
regard the organism as more advanced because early
maturity gives an appearance of superiority. Bright
children are usually classed higher than their more
slowly developing comrades. The mental powers are
especially stimulated by this acceleration, and to
them we give undue weight in determining the relative rank of individuals. A lack of nutrition checks
the growth of a part prematurely and if severe causes
actual decay. The renewal of energy starts the
growth of higher organs and leaves the lower ones in
an incomplete form. A series of changes are thus
made with more than normal rapidity, and a premature development results, followed by an equally
premature old age. The marks of acceleration are
thus the same as those of old age. The resulting
mental powers may for a time indicate superiority,
but this superiority is temporary. Persons so endowed
must therefore be classed as degenerates, even though
they come up to social standards and do not show the
tendency toward vice and crime that is so often manifest in those whose development is retarded through

the overgrowth of lower faculties. In neither case
has normality been reached, and by both the level of
humanity is lowered.

Heredity has no mechanism that determines the
rate of progress. Parts do not stop growing because
of some vital limitation coming from the germ cell.
So long as nutrition is abundant, growth continues.
The only check to growth is a deficit in the nutritive
supplies. New organs stop the growth of older ones
by draining off their supply of vital energy. If the
check comes at the right time, we call the part normal;
but if premature or delayed, the balance of growth is
disturbed and degeneration sets in. Degeneration is
not therefore defective heredity, but growth out of
balance. Heredity determines the direction of progress. The rate of growth as contrasted with its direction is mainly, if not solely, due to the supply of nutrition. A deficit causes parts to lag behind their
normal growth; a surplus pushes them ahead of it.
Both tendencies are usually found in the same organism. By the law of compensation, an overgrowth in
one direction leads to a meagerness in growth in others.
This fact should not cause confusion in the study of
degeneration, because its two causes are easily distinguished and have readily observed effects. Overgrowths we call morbid; for accelerations or the pre-

mature stoppage of growth the best term is senility. Described in this way we get ready objective tests of the kind of degeneration any organism undergoes. If we remember that any growth beyond the normal standard is wrong growth, the morbid becomes merely an extra supply of energy destroying the normal balance of the organism. That morbid growth is cured by the draining of this extra energy, by strenuous exercise or by dieting shows that its basis is in nutrition and not in heredity. Senility is likewise a problem of nutrition. There is no natural old age. Its source is always in some unnecessary restriction of vital processes. Organisms are naturally immortal, not mortal.

I have avoided the moral stigmata of degeneration because they are the effects of the physical characteristics that have been described. Every kind of moral degeneration usually accompanies some kind of physical degeneration and is a function of it. The pressure that disturbs the normal balance of an organism creates morbidity in some parts and senility in others. There are nevertheless two distinct types of immoral action conforming to the two kinds of degeneration. Morbid degeneration shows itself in emotionalism and an excess of passion. It is this type of immorality that first strikes the attention because of its naked opposition to social ends. Emotionalism and passion reveal an existence below the social level, and no society can hold together that does not exert a strong pressure to keep them in subjection. They do not, however, constitute the only manifestation of the anti-social spirit. The egoist with self-centered desires undermines the social spirit quite as effectively as the passion of the morbid degenerate. The line between the selfish and the social is not fixed by heredity nor by the constitution of the mind. It is imposed by the necessities of social existence. The sharper the pressure, the more clearly defined is the contrast between the two, and the more effective is the urgency with which the demands of the ego present themselves. It is often claimed that selfishness is a normal motive and that the social spirit is in some way derived from it. No such derivation is possible, for selfishness is a disintegrating, not a constructive, force. It is easy to go from the social to the non-social, for this is the path of degeneration; but there is no road from selfishness to generosity. The social ego contrasts society with nature. The self-centered ego contrasts society with itself. The distribution of products rather than their acquisition from nature thus gets first place, and all is subordinated to gratifications that meet intense momentary wants.

CHAPTER VIII

SENILE DEGENERATION

VIII

THE preceding discussion should make clear the variety of uses to which the word "degeneration" has been put. Progress consists in relating these uses to one another by separating the fundamental from the casual and by giving the right emphasis to elements that are likely to be overlooked. It is easy to see why defective heredity should have received early attention, for the abnormalities it produces can be readily measured. Such studies were necessarily first in order of time, for without a clear understanding of the relations of higher to lower organisms no scientific research in defects and abnormalities could be made. This knowledge, however, does not solve the problems of degeneration. It only clears the way for more careful study. There are external factors in degeneration, as well as those of heredity, and they produce, not merely reversion to lower types, but changes more truly deserving the name of degeneration. Of these objective causes, nutrition is the most prominent. Its effects, favorable and unfavorable, open up a field of investigation as important as the influences producing atavistic traits. Disturbances in nutrition throw organisms out of balance. In subsequent stages of development some parts have more, and some less, than the normal degree of growth. If growth is superfluous or ill-directed, a part so affected is morbid; if it has less than the normal growth, it is senile. Morbidness is primarily an overflow of energy; senility a loss of vital power. The one leads to disease, the other to decay. They are both found in abnormal persons, because an overflow of energy in one direction leads to its diminution in others. The marks of the two, however, are so distinct that they can readily be separated and studied. Of the two, morbidness is more closely allied to defective heredity, and hence the stigmata of the two are practically the same. Defective heredity is the more deep-seated; the morbidness of over-nutrition shows itself in a stunted development of the higher faculties. Its cause is an arresting of the normal diversion of surplus energy from the lower to the higher organs. Morbidness ends in disease when the local surplus becomes unmanageable; it creates mental abnormalities through indirect effects on the higher powers. Disease, hysteria and insanity are its most pronounced manifestations; but it has so many minor symptoms that its abnormal effects cannot be related to their cause without the most careful study.

[122]

However, so much has been done in this field that a restatement is scarcely needed. Morbidness and defective heredity are overemphasized elements in the study of degeneration. They need further investigation much less than a clear demarcation from other forms of degeneration not so well known.

If cases of defective heredity are isolated from those in which degeneration is due to objective factors, the stigmata of each can be plainly recognized. When causes are objective, the later, more complicated hereditary qualities will be more affected than the earlier, more simple ones. When growth is not progressive, we may be sure some objective factor has come in to deflect it from its normal course. If a child resembles a distant ancestor in all stages of its development, we may assume that a real atavism has occurred and that the cause lies in the germ cell. But if the reversion is only in the later stages of growth or is there more pronounced than in earlier ones, it is reasonable to assume that the growth of the person is out of balance and that its causes are objective. Ancestral resemblance in such cases will be partial, either on the side of morbid growth or of premature arrests in development. Surplus and deficit of nutrition are thus the objective causes of degeneration, and their physical stigmata are a one-sided growth or arrest of growth that deviates more widely from the normal in higher than in lower stages. Morbidness in a part is the physical mark of surplus nutrition. Premature arrest of development is likewise a sure sign of deficient nutrition. This, when continued, creates a condition of senility. The objective causes and physical stigmata of degeneration thus seem easy of recognition and detection. To complete the study, however, we must note also the mental stigmata of degeneration. In at least one aspect, it is easy to do this. The connection between morbidness and emotionalism has often been pointed out. Morbidness is the overgrowth of the lower faculties and the dwarfing of the higher. Emotionalism is waste energy going out in activity instead of growth. Had the higher powers not been arrested in growth, this energy would have been diverted into useful channels. The emotions would then have ceased to be active or at least have been kept under control.

A clearer idea of emotionalism may be gained by referring to its physical basis. Irritability and contractibility are the two elementary manifestations of organic life. Irritability is activity without an end. There is change and often intense excitability without any useful reaction. Contractibility may be said to be organized irritability. The same energy that in a disorganized part creates irritability in a normally organized part effects some definite useful end. The upward change is thus from irritability to contraction. If this higher outlet of energy is created, the emotional manifestation of irritability diminishes or disappears. We are scarcely cognizant of the working of a normal part. There is no waste energy for emotional manifestations. If this be true of the upward tendencies of an organism, the reverse would follow in the case of degeneration. The part acts imperfectly, and contraction degenerates into mere irritation. Surplus energy is kept from its natural outlet and manifests itself in emotion, which, if strong, becomes hysteria. Emotion is thus the effect of waste energy and appears when morbid changes in lower organs check normal activity. It grows with degeneration and disappears beneath the changes that evoke normal growth.

Emotionalism, then, is the mental sign of morbidness and of surplus energy with no effective outlet. What is the corresponding mark of the arrest of development caused by a deficit of energy? Here is a field in which little has been done, and in making a start the same difficulty is encountered that obstructed progress in the study of morbid degeneration. Its fundamental contrast shocks because it unsettles popular beliefs. To say that genius and insanity are allied states, and that the great men of the past have been unbalanced rather than superior minds, seems to border on absurdity. Yet until this plain truth has been driven home the doctrine of degeneration cannot get a hearing. The criterion in this case is not whether genius is useful or is worthy of admiration. Both of these facts may readily be admitted. We may go even further and say that genius is indispensable; that without its rise the history of the world would be a series of ignoble events. The real test is whether a genius is an elevation above the normal or a deviation from it. If all the world were made on his plan, would there be a rise or a fall in the scale of human existence? Only when we answer this question can we recognize the peculiar qualities that ally the genius, of superlative social value, to the insane. Society cannot move upward by acquiring the physical and mental traits of the genius any more than it could by approximating those of the insane. It is not his effect on heredity that gives the genius his place, but the effect he has on society. He disappears and leaves no lineal descendant; but the laws he created, the victories he won, the inventions he made, the books he wrote or the example he set are a precious heritage in which all participate. The gains that come through genius are in the field of acquired traits, and are handed

[126]

down from generation to generation as a social heritage, but not through heredity. His relations to the insane are of no social consequence. Neither he nor they are of the normal group who pass on our physical heredity to coming generations. How normal people become supernormal is a radically different problem from telling how victories are won or inventions made. The one is a problem of heredity; the other belongs to the history of civilization. As civilization advances by social means more than by changes in heredity, a decline in heredity may go along with an increase of civilization and culture. This is what happens when progress comes through heroes instead of through the rise of normal citizens. It is a well-attested generalization that heroes come when the nation they succor is in a state of decline. They are thus the index of a degeneration in race traits even though they give a compensation in higher civilization.

With these facts and analogies in mind it will be easier to approach the problem of the mental stigmata of an arrest of development. At the start a generalization must be made similar to that affirming the close kinship of genius and insanity. Genius is a form of insanity; in like fashion reason is a mark of the senile. I mean by this that the growth and increasing dominance of the reasoning faculty involve a sapping of the vital forces. Just as the genius is insane, so may it be said that the great thinkers — the founders and promoters of intellectual systems — suffer from wasting disease that drains their vitality and forces them out of the channels of normal growth. They show the marks of accelerated growth, have meager physical powers, and lack the plasticity of thought that normal people enjoy. The thinker is born old; like John Stuart Mill, he has no youth. The rational and the senile are so closely allied that any mark of the one can readily be found in the other. They are both arrests of development due to a drain on the vital powers. Neither is normal, nor does either mark the line along which race progress moves. The thinker, like the genius, is worthy of all praise; but it is a civilization of acquired traits that he molds, not the race progress that comes through improved heredity. He helps progress by a social uplift that others enjoy, not by leaving descendants to reap what he has sown. The latter — not the praises of society — is the real test of a normal life.

We are so accustomed to laud reason as the culmination of human powers that an opposing view seems absurd, and to question its supremacy seems to undermine morality as well as rationalism. These objections have a common origin. The superiority of reason is based on a contrast between the emotional and the rational. A long race struggle has established this supremacy and the morality that goes with it. That the rationalist is less likely to indulge in emotional vices may readily be granted. So, also, it may be freely admitted that calculated indirect action is more effective than the emotional and direct variety. It is not, therefore, the superiority of reason over emotion that is questioned in this view. It is urged merely that reason is not a final stage of human development; that future progress in race qualities does not find its goal in the dominance of reason.

To get this thought clearly before the reader, we must refer again to the contrast between natural and acquired characters. Civilization is objective, and its growth depends upon the ascendancy of acquired traits. Race progress, however, depends on improvement in natural characters. If race progress is checked by growth of civilization, we have degeneration of physique accompanied by social improvements. This is what happens with the dominance of rationalism. Mental progress is an economy; race progress is a growth. The increase of economy is limited, while the growth in energy, if kept along normal lines, may be perpetual. The dominance of economy indicates a diminution of energy; while it brings real gains, it is a mark of physical decline. That the rational attitude

x

is an index of decline in energy is illustrated by the increasing hold it has on men as they grow old. When a man passes the prime of life, physical vigor declines. Economy thus becomes more prominent, until in old age it is supreme. If rationalism and senility grow together, it suggests that they have a common origin. That senility is a waning of energy, everyone knows. If it can be shown that growth in thinking powers has the same origin, many mysteries hitherto unsolved can be explained.

The plastic cell or organ has within it many possibilities of activity. At the same time there is a lack of definiteness in the direction activity may take. As maturity approaches, possible directions of activity decrease in number and grow in definiteness. The useful movements are often repeated and each repetition brings greater ease of execution; less useful, sporadic acts become more and more difficult. Energy thus flows along fixed lines and activity becomes determined. As the flow of energy diminishes with age, activity falls into ruts. Varied activity becomes increasingly difficult, and ultimately impossible. Lack of choice is thus a lack of energy and plasticity. As old age approaches, the line of least resistance is so well established that there is no difficulty in forecasting the conduct. Failure of energy is the cause of the determinism of old age, not any set direction to activity given to the organism by its heredity. Every cell gets at birth a plasticity and susceptibility that is lost only as energy fails.

Few would deny these facts, I think, if they were applied only to energy in its bodily form. The principle is too patent to be gainsaid. Objection is more likely to arise when it is urged that thought is a consequence of bodily activity, that it follows the same laws and is limited by the same conditions. Perhaps this cannot be proved by direct observation; but it can at least be shown that changes take place in thought, as old age approaches, analogous to those that accompany declining energy. Belief is active and easy in youth: the viewpoint is fixed in old age. When maturity is reached it becomes increasingly difficult to change opinions, and in old age it is practically impossible to do so. This suggests that plasticity in thought and action have the same basis, and that they grow and decline under similar conditions. Opinions are not unchangeable because of their logic, but because the brain cells that form the physical basis have lost their plasticity, and hence cannot make new combinations. The once accepted must be retained because there is a failure of surplus energy to force new associations. Ideas become inseparable in thought because

the mind has not the energy to sever them. Unity
of ideas, therefore, is no evidence of the unity of underlying phenomena, nor does it afford any test of the
constitution of the mind. The ability to make dis-
tinctions is merely an index of the amount of effective
energy the organism possesses, and of the plasticity
of its cells. If the number of inseparable ideas grows
with age, and if there is no difference in the power exerted over the mind by late acquired and early acquired
associations, there is no reason why explanations should
be sought for one group that are plainly not needed
for the other. The pressure of a deficit unifies the
action of each subordinated organ, and the degree of
definiteness increases as this pressure grows. Instinctive action is an extreme form of this pressure. Here
the activity of a group of nerve centers is so fully
determined that one well-recognized action follows
their awakening. We think of fixed ideas as a stigma
of the insane; yet all of us have fixed ideas stamped
on our thinking. The difference is that our fixed ideas
are useful and theirs are injurious. There is no difference, however, in the mode of acquiring them or of
the mechanism under which they act.

Determined action and fixed ideas are not the product of any mechanism of heredity, nor are they due
to the constitution of the mind. They have their

origin in objective conditions that act through the pressure created by a deficit of energy. It is not the completeness of the germinal elements in heredity, but the lack of them, that makes determinate action possible. A moth does not fly towards a light because of an inherited mechanism impelling this action. If its mechanism were more complete it could fly away from the light as easily as to approach it. The action of light and heat make up for the defects of heredity, and impel a definite action where otherwise no fixed reaction would take place. The simple reactions due to a deficit are equally objective, and help, as do tropisms, to make up for the incompleteness of heredity. On a simple heredity it is thus possible to build a complex organism that meets the most varied conditions. We do not need mechanisms when objective forces can be made to effect the same ends.

CHAPTER IX

THE WILL

IX

THE problem of religion is to make clear the relation of degeneration to the will, and to show how the evils of degeneration may be replaced by upbuilding tendencies. Degeneration is almost universal, because every disturbance in the balance of growth and all defects in nutrition depress the individual affected below his normal level. Subsequent growth does not remedy these defects, but tends to exaggerate them. If development is retarded, morbid degeneration sets in, which ends in emotionalism, hysteria or insanity. If development is accelerated, senile degeneration results. This carries with it rigidity of parts and dominance of instinctive, imitative and egoistic tendencies. With heredity and the nutritive processes left to themselves, an organism can scarcely fail to fall into one or the other of these pitfalls. Some other force must be evoked if the narrow path of normal progress is to be followed to a stable goal in a higher life. What is this force and how does it effect its ends?

Action is either the result of antecedent conditions working from the outside, or it is merely the expression of some internal reaction. Acts are determinate, not because of any general law of universal causation, but because some evolutionary process has eliminated less effective ways of procedure. Determinism is a goal, not a first principle. We reach it by growth and change, not through primary forces or predetermined causes. It has as many forms as there are independent sources of activity, and we become wholly determinate only as all of these are harmonized and coördinated.

There are two kinds of determinism so prominent that they cannot fail to attract attention. Biologic determinism covers the whole range of heredity. Organic change follows definite laws, and its principles are capable of definite enunciation. The germ cell has various potentialities that work themselves out in organic development and become manifest in every normal being. Were all characters natural and all acts instinctive, there would be no field left indeterminate by biologic evolution. The contrast of natural and acquired characters is a recognition that there are many acts not directly controlled by heredity. Acquired characters must of necessity have some other source and they grow in importance as organisms rise in the scale of being. They indicate some form of external determinism which supplements or displaces the biologic determinism of lower organisms. I cannot enter an exhaustive discussion of external determinism; but one aspect of it is so prominent that, if not the sole form, it may be taken as a type of all others. Economic determinism acts through nutrition and other external objects that each organism must exert itself to secure. The principle of economy is back of all acquired traits, activities and knowledge. Their force, however exerted, makes the economic determinism that stands in contrast with the biologic determinism imposed by heredity. The two are dominant forces in man's determinate life; but they are not the sole factors. The third is the will. Its workings cannot be understood until the earlier and more objective forms of control have their activity explained. To call an act one of will when the forces of biologic selection or economic pressure are operative, confuses what otherwise would be a plain problem. If these two great forces cover the whole field, there is no will in any sense worth investigating. The will is a reality when there are acts free from the pressure of either of these forces. If we can get beyond heredity and beyond the pressure of economic events there is a reality to freedom that it is worth a struggle to realize.

What, then, is the essence of these two great forces, and how can we know when we have passed beyond the realm of their activity? Biologic determinism is the tendency in organic life to repeat the stages of development through which predecessors have gone. This constant repetition is the essence of biological heredity; and in so far as it is active, determinate action results. Economic determinism, however, is due not to a positive, but to a negative principle. Regular action is acquired as any part is brought under the pressure of a deficit. Plastic action is indeterminate and may move in any direction. Lessen the plasticity and action becomes more fixed in kind and less open to variation in its results. Complete determinism arises when a long-standing deficit has reduced action to its simplest form. Senile life loses all spontaneity, and a routine is established as complete as that due to organic heredity. Biologic determinism is static, for its results never vary except under morbid influences. Economic determinism may be retrogressive, for the pressure of deficit lowers the tone of an organism and forces it out of the normal path. No matter how great the economy, and hence the immediate advantage, loss of energy and of plasticity have no compensations that keep an organism from stagnation and decay. The best that could come from complete biologic and economic determinism would be a static condition. We must look elsewhere for the principles of progress. These lie in some indeterminate field outside the province of these two great forces.

A closer examination reveals the missing element and shows how it works. What checks the growth of the lower parts of an organism and thus makes for the the appearance of higher powers is not any result of the principles of heredity nor of any germ determinant that limits growth. It is the appearance of new organs turning surplus energy in other directions that keeps older parts true to their normal development. Parts remain normal only when they are under the pressure of a deficit. Then only does biologic determinism keep their growth in the right direction and economic determinism force them to function in useful ways. No organ will grow normally and become a useful agent in survival with a surplus of energy to disturb the regularity of its action. Normal growth and activity continue only so long as new parts appear to drain off this surplus through the indeterminate activity which youth and plasticity stimulate. The useful parts are the older ones acting under the pressure of deficit. It is the mere activity of the newer part, not its direction, function or regularity, that aids the organism.

Indeterminate action is thus an essential element in normal growth. Without it, the organism degenerates either in a morbid, or in a senile direction. It gives to the partially formed and more plastic higher powers a function in the place of what would otherwise be mere waste. We must, however, call it indeterminate with a qualification. It is indeterminate in relation to survival, but not in relation to distant ends and better adjustment. Without the activity it promotes, future normal growth would be prevented, and the possibility of better adjustment denied. It can, therefore, be called telic determinism; for it creates adjustments by opening up the line of future progress and by keeping organisms true to it. The formless activity of to-day through the growth of still higher parts is put under the pressure of deficit. Activity thereby becomes fixed in direction and determinate in purpose. Each newer part in turn presses its predecessors into practical use and takes on itself the function of regulating them through new expressions of indeterminate action that exhaust the stock of surplus energy.

This office of using up surplus energy and thus promoting the normal activity of lower parts is the primary function of the will. It is not an immaterial something, nor a form of higher thought, but is the active expression of a partially formed, newer organ, with much plasticity and of no immediate use. The will is not the source of clear definite thought, nor is it the place where controlling motives arise. Thoughts come from the intellect: motives arise through the emotions. These are both within the realm of determinate action. They result from the action of the older and less plastic parts from which surplus of energy has been withdrawn. Volition keeps growth normal. When this happens, the much admired constituents of thought and activity work out their normal destiny, keep mankind progressive and make its collective efforts telic. We move forward, not by conscious individual efforts directed toward survival, but by the social results of activity that has no immediate end. If pure thought and utilitarian motives absorbed all of our energy, progress would cease and degradation begin.

The will is thus the expression of a movement from plastic to definite action, taking place when the higher centers are forming. We should think of mental activity not as the result of a definitely constituted organ with specific and well defined parts, but rather of a series of organs, some newly and partially made, some normal and others in process of decay. Older parts are gradually thrown off or absorbed. Newer parts increase in the regularity and effectiveness of their acts as their growth rounds them out and makes them capable of performing the functions of older decaying parts. The rise of a species in the scale of being depends on keeping up this series of changes by discarding old parts and by reducing new ones to regular and useful forms of activity. The changes are progressive so long as new parts absorb the surplus energy and force their predecessors into a compact group with related activities.

Two difficulties prevent a clear concept of the will. The first is that it is thought of as immaterial and hence without the physical background of other faculties. The second is that we confuse moral judgments with volitions. With passion and intellectual activity we recognize the relation between the mental state and its physical antecedents. By this means, passion and intellect can be readily contrasted and their province made clear. The will has no such method of recognition, and hence it is confused with matters of habit, of passion, of intellect or any other propensity that happens for the moment to command attention. This indefiniteness must be set aside in the interest of clear thought. We must think of the physical antecedents of the will as clearly as we do of other native powers and faculties. This antecedent is surplus energy. Without vigor all acts are routine not involving volition. The will is mind made active by surplus energy; the intellect is the mind acting under a deficit; passion is the mind controlled by its inherited mechanisms. The intellect gets its force through the acquired characters that are objective in their origin. Passion is a matter of heredity. It is the surplus of energy above the demands of heredity and environment that makes volition possible. Volition should therefore be associated with strenuous, and not with moral, acts. Most moral acts are habits and do not involve our highest powers. Although valuable, they give no index of the uplift that presses society forward to new goals. It is the telic tendencies of surplus energy that produce epoch-making social changes. The best measure of this force is to be had in sports, athletic contests and sudden emergencies that call forth all the powers of a man. It is the will of the athlete, not his physical powers, that gives him the victory. If we looked to him for example of volition, instead of looking to the moral recluse, we should have no difficulty in separating acts of volition from those of the intellect.

Determinate action is not fixed in amount, but varies with the energy of a man and the plasticity of his brain cells. Men may be said to have two wills, the one a will to believe, which manifests itself when they feel energetic, and the other a will to criticize, which is potent when they lack energy. A surplus of energy puts them in one mood, while a deficit evokes the other. Most men shift back and forth from one mood to the other as their surplus energy varies and their health improves or fails. It breaks no law to change from one of these conditions to the other, since the cause lies either in objective conditions, a nervous shock or some new inspiration. Men are less determinate in youth than in old age, and also less so in action than in thought. The young of each generation are forced to think in old forms by their elders, while their activities are shaped by their own experience. Thought is thus more determinate than activity, and from this difference arises the struggle between belief and doubt, so much emphasized by religious experience.

Freedom is not the power to do what one pleases, but the power to throw off depression and abnormalities. It demands not the absence of control over individual acts, but the power of a thorough regeneration. Volition, rightly understood, is the antecedent of regeneration, not of acts performed by the parts of the brain and body that have acquired definite functions. Its essence is the exciting of activity among a new group of brain cells, and the doing there of acts hitherto performed in an older part. If all the brain had definite functions set by heredity, no change of this sort could be made. If, on the other hand, men in their ordinary actions use but a fraction of their brain cells, only this fraction will be definitely enough organized to be the seat of regular functions. The unused cells can be made active by the presence of surplus energy, and this activity once begun may replace that of older parts with well defined functions. The possibility of regeneration exists if mental activity can be transferred from one part of the brain to another. Such a change demands surplus energy, plastic cells and some extraordinary event to fix the attention and to arouse activity.

When these three are in conjunction, marked transformations of nervous activity and of mental concepts result. The social process is so much more dominant in thought than is heredity, that when a break is once made, a thorough reconstruction of ideas and motives is possible. Regeneration does not alter heredity. It uses hereditary forces in a new way to modify the action of the social process that controls thought. It is no more a violation of the uniformity of nature than a mutation is a deviation from organic law. Any striking combination of events makes changes in development that perpetuate themselves and thus prevent a return to the former equilibrium. Regeneration is an extraordinary event, but not in any way marvelous. It is supernormal, but not supernatural. Men do not violate the laws of nature by rising above the normal any more than they do when they sink below it. Volition is more than activity. It is activity among plastic cells forced on by the action of surplus energy. By making will the psychic antecedent of regeneration instead of an immaterial entity, religion avoids an impassable philosophic barrier, and realizes an opportunity to verify its claims by evidence that no careful thinker will reject.

CHAPTER X

CHARACTER

X

It is an error to think of the mind as having a definite constitution either in a material or in an immaterial sense. It is not a unit with definite, predetermined expressions, but is a series of developing functions forced into an imperfect unity by organic growth and external pressure. In the growth of any being, the earlier parts or stages are constantly disappearing through disuse, metamorphosis and other means of organic transformation. In their places come new organs that do in better ways the acts performed by their disappearing predecessors in the chain of organic growth. Life and its functions are at no time confined to any one of these links, but are aggregated in several of them. A moving equilibrium is created that, with losses and gains, takes the organism upward through the series of changes demanded by its destiny. Each new link has in it the same inherited possibilities. It has neither more nor less than its predecessors had, but antecedent growth and external pressure force it to take on peculiar functions that complement those of other organic parts. Its potentialities are thus developed or suppressed. With no other heredity than its predecessors, it may grow in new ways and manifest distinctive qualities.

Mind, as we find it in human beings, has qualities that have developed at these stages or levels. Three of these stages are so apparent that they can readily be distinguished. The lowest level is seen mainly in the instincts and emotions; the second is the intellect; the third is the will. Of these the intellect is the normal level, for through it our effective adjustments are made. The instinctive and emotional level is plainly subnormal, for if we allow ourselves to be controlled by its impulses, we degenerate. The will is the supernormal level. It is here that new adjustments and fresh thought take their rise. It differs from the lower levels not in kind nor in its possibilities, but in the fact that it is more plastic and that much of its activity is still indeterminate. Its primary function is to be active, not to perform specific tasks directly advantageous in survival. By absorbing surplus energy it keeps the lower faculties normal and thus adds to their effective power. This indeterminateness is the cause of the effectiveness of the lower organs. It thus gives the appearance of a greater regularity of action than exists. Only in the subnormal or degenerating parts is the reign of law complete. Elsewhere there is plas-

[152]

ticity and indefiniteness of action and of results. This is the essence of growth and from it the genetic concept of life takes its rise.

This view of the mind could readily be illustrated in many ways, but the concept is clear enough for present purposes. Indeed, to some it may too clearly point to the conclusion that it is at bottom the old material view of life so often rejected by the leaders of religious thought. There is an element of truth in this, — enough to confuse many readers, — but there is also an important difference. The material concept of the mind originated when chemistry was the leading science. Using its principles as analogies, psychologists separated the contents of the mind into elements similar to those found in chemical analysis. The mind was thought of as a crucible in which strange results sprang from a few elements. In this way a definiteness of construction was given to the mind that was satisfying in its completeness, but it failed to give a clew to the mind's real origin or functions. A static mind built from external elements, and a genetic mind constantly rebuilt by its own forces and antecedents, are radically different concepts. A genetic mind has material elements, but they are subordinate to the mental life and are constantly rebuilt by it. This life comes from these elements, but is not of them. The genetic always has some indeterminate factors permitting the reshaping of the whole as its growth advances. Older parts give way to newer ones, molded not by the material elements in their predecessors, but by their mental life. In each new growth the physical is less dominant and the mental more nearly supreme. We cannot escape the material, but we need not be controlled by it.

The genetic view of mind, instead of setting up concepts and deducing principles antagonistic to religion, emphasizes the same facts and reaches the same conclusions. Both emphasize an indeterminate element in conduct. Through this, choices are made and the possibility is afforded of reconstructing thought and motive in ways that make for higher life. They also have in common the fact that control by the will is mainly through acquired traits and sentiments. If all forces acting on the will were natural and predetermined, there could not be the prevailing emphasis on the educating and strengthening of the will now found in religious literature. It makes this same thought emphatic to say that the will is plastic and is shaped by present conditions, not by predecessors in time and space. There is also a like emphasis on the danger and prevalence of degeneration. Through retardation the lower levels of the mind may remain too strong to be controlled by their legitimate masters in the more plastic parts of the mind;

[154]

or through premature acceleration the intellect may so fully control the emotions that a selfish mental attitude asserts itself. Finally, and most important, is the thought of regeneration by which the old passes away and the new comes to its full vigor. To be born again is an old religious theme. The genetic organism is constantly being reorganized. Older parts fall into decay or are cast off. Newer parts take over the functions of their predecessors. In other ways and under new conditions they restore what is lost and elevate the whole organism to a higher plane. The genetic mind has its levels as well as the organism of which it is a part. In normal growth the lower ones are constantly repressed, and decay through disuse. There is thus a shifting of control to the will; the mind in consequence is made over fully enough to be the psychical expression of the new birth sought by religion.

This viewpoint, whether taught by religion or psychology, emphasizes the importance of character. If the higher levels of the mind were not plastic, if their nature were predetermined by the germ cell or by the structure of the lower levels, our acts would be the results of past, not of present conditions. Without plasticity there could be no growth in character. Hence there could be no way for education to mold or for religion to regenerate. Growth in character is possible to the extent that the acquired powers of the will dominate over natural traits. The lower levels of thought and action whose activities are predetermined must be suppressed; their structure must waste away through disuse and their energy be absorbed in the newer activities of the will. The decay of the old and predetermined must go hand in hand with the formation of acquired traits in the plastic parts of the brain. The will becomes definite in its action by assuming the functions that in cruder ways the lower levels of the mind have hitherto performed.

This transfer of function and control is the essence of every uplift. When we see its effects we call it growth in character, and we think of some immaterial change as its cause. Could we measure the physical changes in the structure of the brain as readily as we note their effects on the activity of men we would see that the one is as real as the other and that both are indications of the reconstructive process accompanying normal growth. The old decays; the new increases in definiteness. It takes on itself the burden of organic control and the responsibility for the continuance of vital processes. It matters little whether we think of these changes as mental or physical; as growth in character or in organic function. The vital point is: the decay of the old and the growth of the new, the loss of control naturally predetermined and the gain in control through acquired traits, the transfer of functions from old, well established parts to those that are plastic and fresh.

By these means the well-recognized levels of the mind get the order of their importance reversed. The naturally dominant emotions and instincts become subordinated to the acquired traits of the will. On the lower level, the emotions and the instincts are an expression of the predetermined direction in which its activity moves. They are, however, in a process of decay. The organism would lose its adjustment, if other forms of determined action were not devised. The intellectual level lies in the mental powers created by the pressure of deficit. Its objective expression is the social process that supplements mental activity, rounds out its limitations and makes the laws that give force to all of its expressions. What the instincts and emotions are to the organic level, and the social process is to the intellectual level, character is to the will. It changes plasticity and mere activity into definite reactions which create adjustments and replace the control formerly exercised by the emotions and intellect. There is in this change nothing new. All that is peculiar to will-power lies in the constitution of any organic part. The same change of function from lower to higher levels has often before taken place. Decay and growth have always been active.

The new is plastic and the old doomed to decay. The difference is not in this, but in the completeness of the changes involved. From an almost complete state of predeterminateness, in which natural characters and external pressure are dominant, a new control arises that is largely plastic. In so far as it is predetermined, conditions are made by the pressure of the social process to a far greater degree than by organic antecedents. Emotions and instincts are thus displaced by abstract mental concepts and social ideals. These are the mold in which character is shaped. A man of will should have no natural emotions or inherited instincts strong enough to control him. Their decay is the condition on which his strength of character depends.

If the will is a mental level and character an index of the reconstructions by which activities are controlled, a new importance is given to the relation of higher to lower levels and to the means by which transferences of control from one to another are carried through. It now becomes necessary to trace the physical antecedents of thought. The decay or disuse of organs must precede the reconstruction of mental life. The shifting of growth from one part of an organism to others must reorganize the mental phenomena their activity evokes. As the instincts and emotions arise from the level where decay and reconstruction are most evident, it is to them we must turn in looking for the connection between mental facts and vital processes. To most writers the emotions and instincts seem unrelated. Discussions throw little light either on the relations of instincts and emotions to each other or to the underlying vital mechanism. I have found but one writer [1] who recognizes a direct connection between instincts and emotions. The relation he finds is not the same as suggests itself to me, but the start he makes is an intelligent one. Mr. McDougall thinks that each of the principal instincts presupposes some kind of emotional excitement, so that its activity is always accompanied by the emotion peculiar to it. The emotion, if I understand him rightly, is the mental expression of those organic facts whose effects we call instinctive. Instinct and emotion would then grow and decay together, and be strong or weak from the same group of vital conditions. To me, another connection seems more probable. I would say that instead of growing and decaying together, the growth of emotion is an index of decay in the instinct it accompanies.

To make my meaning clear and to give a clew to my reasoning, I shall first state the general principle on which it is based. An instinct is the mark of effective activity; a condition in which energy goes out fully in

[1] See McDougall, "Social Psychology," Chap. III.

activity. The instinctive act is the most perfect of organic adjustments, and in it the amount of work done is proportionate to the energy at the disposal of the past. Were all acts instinctive, mental phenomena might be clear, but they would not be emotional. The instinct to keep an upright position under normal conditions hardly enters into consciousness. When it is so weakened that we fear a fall, it may be the source of a strong emotion.

I would not say with Mr. McDougall that a dog barks in pursuit of game because it has a social instinct, but because its whole energy is not used up in the pursuit. The aroused but unused energy flows over to other centers and awakens their activity. It is an old saying that barking dogs never bite. I would interpret this to mean that a biting dog is more instinctive, and that all his energy goes out in activity. The instinct of the barking dog partially fails, and the aroused energy is used up in barking instead of biting. The domesticated dog has degenerated from the earlier condition, where energy and activity were coördinated. Energy flows as in olden times, but the partial disuse of his organs of pursuit makes an overflow of energy that is exhibited in other parts as emotion. A squirrel that buries nuts lacks emotion about them. The activity runs its course instinctively, with so close a correspondence between energy and activity that no surplus remains to generate feeling. The instinct of flight is not of necessity accompanied by fear. If the instinct works perfectly, there is no emotion. The act of flight absorbs the energy and puts the animal in a position free from danger. It is the imperfect working of the instinct that evokes fear. This emotion has its seat, not in the centers made active in flight, but in other parts to which the overflow of energy goes.

The use of the emotion is that it arouses these related parts and forces them to come to the aid of the instinctive activities. Under emotion, either the whole organism acts, or many more of its powers are made effective than is the case where an act is purely instinctive. Emotional activity is more complex than instinctive action. It arises when the organic mechanisms are being displaced by the more conscious coördinations of the higher centers. The old must to some extent decay to permit this change. The less effective action of the old leaves free a fund of energy that is used up in arousing related parts. The resulting emotion concentrates the attention on the instinctive act and brings to its aid the whole conscious force of the organism. The newer parts thus become trained to do the work of their decaying predecessors and action is raised to a higher level through the increase of its conscious elements. Emotion is thus the mental sign of waste energy. Instinct indicates efficiency. When it alone operates, the potential energy of the part and the amount of work done exactly correspond. While emotion is waste energy, it is of use in arousing related parts and in centering the attention on the instinctive act, thus bringing the whole organism into action. As a stage in development emotion indicates that older parts are decaying, and that their activity is being taken over by the higher, more plastic centers.

Emotion has a suggestive power that makes the activity of newly formed organs definite. These in consequence follow more closely in the line of their predecessors. It is this suggestive power that gives the emotions their greatest power. In every organic transition due to the creation of new parts and the decay of the old they bind the two together, keep up the continuity of the organism and shape the new in harmony with the old. They cease to operate only when the reorganization is so complete that the whole energy of the organism might go out in new ways as effectually as in the old. This point, however, never comes; for the process of reconstruction and advance is continuous. There is always decay to create emotion, and there are always new parts for it to direct. It is thus shifted from part to part and expresses itself in new ways in each epoch of organic growth. Its emphasis on organic needs is the primary force that arouses the will to action. Were it the only force, the problem of the will would be simple. Each new part, as it developed in determinateness, would repeat the selfsame activities to which its predecessors were accustomed. The opposing force comes from what we call character. Impulses and passions are natural emotions whose direction is determined by the organs in which they arise. The character elements are sentiments that stand in close relation to the intellect, where acquired traits take their rise. These sentiments are social in origin. On them we rely to stem the tide of rising impulse and passion.

To explain the will is to show how these newly acquired sentiments dominate in men over the more powerful impulses that through heredity control the organism. We get a solution of this difficulty, not by thinking of the will as an immaterial force, but as a plastic expression of forces determinate only in so far as they have been organized as social sentiments. When a conflict comes between acquired sentiments and natural impulses, the will acts with the sentiments and against the impulses. To say this is not to restate the problem in other words, but to divide it into two parts. The moral education of a man might be complete and his social sentiments strong. Yet, if he had no surplus energy to reënforce them, they would be powerless in a conflict with impulse and passion. The indeterminate forces of the will are an index of surplus energy. If men were normal, every lower part would be under the pressure of deficit. All surplus energy would be concentrated in the plastic parts as a reserve force to be used when the sentiments arouse its activity. What the strength of the moral sentiments is, and what is the amount of surplus energy, are two distinct problems. The one depends on education and the other on the physical normality of the man. There can be no effective volition if surplus energy is absent. Its action, if present, would be indeterminate without the growth of moral sentiments. If it acts with the acquired sentiments and against natural impulses, we can be sure that normal people will act right if properly educated. It becomes doubly sure in the case of degenerates that they will act from impulse and not from education. Hence the need of the opposition to degeneration which is the essence of religious activity.

CHAPTER XI

INSPIRATION

XI

THE most difficult of religious topics is yet to be discussed. It is difficult, not from any intrinsic reason, but because religious people distrust scientific analysis. If one religiously inclined states his experience, he finds that he has gained nothing by a frank confession. He will more likely feel a loss of self-respect by recognizing the similarities between what to him is sacred and what is plainly a degenerate state in those with whom he is compared. Inspiration is an emotional state and shows the peculiarities of other emotions. Abnormalities do not follow distinct laws of their own. They are merely exaggerations which, because of their striking features, can be more easily studied than can the less obtrusive normal phenomena from which they are differentiated and derived. The road to the knowledge of the normal is through the abnormal. Only after the abnormal symptoms of emotion are well understood can they be separated from religious emotions and the ways pointed out by which the latter may be developed.

If inspiration is normal and not a fancy, it is possible to show how its force and its frequency may be increased. What is more important, it is possible to help others develop inspirational moods and to get the advantage that flows from them. At present our methods of propagating religious ideas are sadly deficient. Until other means are found of helping people to intensify their spiritual convictions, religion will continue in the state of decline so evident in recent years. Any cause fights a losing battle that does not win converts. Our vital experience dies with us unless revived by others. It ceases to have value as evidence unless it be made a matter of heritage. We must therefore analyze religious feelings to get the key to their revival in others. Seeming losses will be transmuted into gains if in the end sound methods of propagating religious feeling are found and used.

To realize this advantage, we must utilize the genetic concept of the mind which has been presented. The mind is not a unit with an innate constitution and a multitude of derived consequences. It is a series of growths, each with the same organic background. These function in different ways because of differences in antecedent conditions and external pressure. There are plastic indeterminate parts, and those falling into decay. Every one has a normal level where action is effective, a subnormal level where degeneration has begun, and a supernormal level, — too plastic to have its action predetermined and too incompletely formed to displace its predecessors in their useful, well-established acts. The forward movements of the organism, however, consist in displacing these decaying parts or in limiting the scope of their activity. This process increases the functions and definiteness of action of the newer parts. Thus readjustments to the environment are made and a high standard of efficiency attained.

This view assumes practical value when we regard the will as the supernormal element, thus separating it from the intellectual process of which it is usually regarded a part. The will thus becomes the seat of surplus energy, the only part in the normal man where surplus dominates. The instincts and animal emotions are in a state of organic decay while the intellect is under the pressure of deficit. The action of the will thus has distinguishing characteristics which enable us to determine what are true volitions in contrast with the impulses coming from the lower organs. Both types of action figure in consciousness. They seem so much alike that we think of all action as willed. They differ radically, however, in their background. Impulses come from below and are marked by their organic origin, or they arise from the external pressure that evokes the action of the intellect. In the one case they are instincts, emotions and passions; in the other they are utilities having force through the values they create. In both cases action is determinate and readily referable to the external causes in which it originates. These organic, economic and social impulses make up the great mass of our acts. We should contrast them in their totality with true volitions which come from the will and hence are free from the pressure, organic or external, that makes them measurable forces.

The first essential in grasping this contrast is to realize that volition takes its rise, not in reason, but in surplus energy. The will does not act on experience or proof, but from a primary impulse aroused by free energy. Its usefulness is not in what it does, but in the absorption of energy that keeps the lower organs normal by forcing them to work under a deficit. The start of volition is thus in energy; its end is in a sentiment. Any repeated act gains emotional power, and thus an impulse is generated that acts like other impulses in a steady, persistent manner toward given ends. At any moment the force of the will lies in the sentiments that its repeated acts have formed. So long, then, as surplus energy flows normally through the will, there is a growth of acquired sentiments and an increase in their dominance over natural impulses. Once check the flow of surplus energy and character degenerates. Control then becomes emotional or intellectual. In the latter case, senile traits steadily increase until old age comes on, with its rigidity of thought and action. Volition is thus a definite process, beginning in surplus of energy and ending in sentiments. If this be granted, we can hope to explain what gives volitions their direction.

First of all, I shall enunciate a principle that will clarify our view of essentials. Reason has no direct influence on the will. Its influence is corrective, not formative. Volition makes sentiments and through them beliefs. Reason chooses between beliefs, but it originates nothing. It merely decides between thoughts and opinions already formed. Reason is an expression of deficit and gets its force by weeding out what some more original power creates. Between the many different directions in which indeterminate activity goes out, it forces choices which make volition seem to be its product instead of its superior. In the virgin soil of a plastic mind beliefs grow lavishly. They are not the result of evidence nor of experience, but of rapid organic growth. To act is to believe. In this state of mind the young go along until they stumble on some limitation arising from lack of energy. Then beliefs begin to clash. The weaker go to the wall, for they are least capable of resisting the pressure of deficit. When we pride ourselves in getting the greatest return for the least effort, we are plainly under the pressure of want and far from that primal state where energy dominates. The utilitarian cramps our concepts so much that we lose sight of our earlier, more energetic state. We even go so far as to esteem personal relics of it as marks of degeneration. These latter states are more effective, but they are neither higher nor primal. We must look in some other quarter than reason to find their source. It is also plain that if surplus energy and its plastic manifestations are the source from which new thought arises, children are more normal than their elders. Their simple faith is nearer the source of inspiration and of new thought than is the logic of later years. With them to think is to act. Simple suggestion is transformed into action by the force of the surplus within them. To act is to create a sentiment in favor of the action. This tends toward its repetition and increase in power. Suggestion is thus the intermediary between surplus energy and sentiment. It is the force that gives direction to the activities of the will and gradually transforms them from indeterminate to determinate action.

It is customary to think of suggestion as a lower, rather than a higher, power. This is because it was first brought into prominence by the study of degenerate types. It is regarded as a force appearing when the normal action of the higher faculties is interrupted.

INSPIRATION

This fact should not cause us to disparage its origin, but should help us to classify the various forms of suggestion and thus bring them into contrast with the pressure of deficit that all intellectual action manifests. Where plasticity and surplus exist, suggestion forestalls the rational process which acts with precision only when plasticity and surplus fail. The degenerate goes wrong not because the power arousing action is of a low nature, but because his ill-balanced condition makes adjustive acts impossible. The child who is led by suggestion would also be eliminated but for the protection of his elders. Even the man of genius is not safe unless he keeps himself out of places where the struggle for life is severe. Suggestion is not so perfect a tool as reason, but it is the original shaping power in plastic minds. When it leads to the creation of senti-ments it is a potent force for progress, the only one that moves in the right direction. When new situations stimulate an unexpected and extraordinary manifestation, or when an unforeseen social situation arises, reason, forethought and prudence fail to give a solution. Suggestion must replace them. The narrow, safe path of reason is surrounded on all sides by the diverging paths of suggestion. These often lead into difficulty, but they may also open the road to a better life.

Two forms of suggestion are obviously useful. Organic suggestion is the power over our plastic higher faculties exercised by the definite impulses of our lower nature. It is suggestion that in the decay of older organs induces the newer ones to take on their activity. There would be no link between the old and the new by which normal progress arises if this force of suggestion were not felt and its dictates followed. Social suggestion is equally prominent. We see it on its bad side when a mob overthrows social law and eagerly follows ways that are crude but energetic. We see it, however, much more frequently on its good side when it strengthens social usage and keeps men within the bounds of law and morality. For much of the good men do they can give no adequate reason. The influence of others, through precept and example, determines acts more frequently than men realize. If we were careful to distinguish suggestion from reason, the dominance of suggestion even in normal men would be evident. It directs surplus energy toward its ends and is never absent except when men fall into the grip of old age.

From the standpoint of religion neither of these well-recognized forms of suggestion is of use. They are more likely to repress religious expression than to evoke its higher manifestations. Organic suggestion gives force to passions. Social suggestion strengthens routine discipline in ways that kill the spirit, even though it may save the letter of the law. The prophet who seeks inspiration subdues organic suggestion by a meager diet, and avoids social suggestion by a life of solitude. In this he is wise, for both organic and social suggestion must be displaced before natural suggestion can begin its forceful but disruptive activity. All men feel the stimulating, suggestive power of nature. They realize that their best thoughts are evoked when under its influence. Given surplus energy as a condition, and nature as an environment, these forces are at a maximum that guide and elevate our thought. Sentiments are thus created that become a bulwark against depression when routine living is once more resumed. It is this state that is the essence of inspiration. When we feel it our religious sentiments grow. As a result we are raised above the normal and substitute distant for immediately useful ends.

It would be useless to analyze religious inspiration unless we also show ways by which consciously to attain it. The transformation of inspiration from an accidental to a social force depends on the creating of regular avenues of approach. The full development of this province is a task larger than I can undertake, but there are some facts whose bearing is so plain that they should not be neglected. Suggestion is an offshoot of surplus energy. When vital forces are at a minimum or on a downward curve, all energy is exhausted in performing the mechanical operations that sustain life. Under these conditions the instincts, emotions, rational thought and like expressions of deficit dominate too fully to permit any waste of energy along untried lines. An upward curve of energy gives the freedom from mechanical control that makes volition possible, and favors conditions that evoke suggestion. Most men are subject to irregularities in their supply of energy. Sickness, disaster, bad food, and many other conditions produce this result. In consequence, most men at intervals pass from one extreme to the other. Downward curves bring doubt, fear and depression; upward curves create men anew and give the higher powers an unwonted supply of energy. It is during the dominance of the upward movement that suggestion is potent and new beliefs are readily formed. The many plans of recent origin for the suppression of pain and the inculcation of invigorating belief have their bases in this thought, even if the mode of expressing it is so immaterial that the physical background of the mind is ignored. To keep the thought of pain out of the mind when depression tends to make it vivid, and to utilize the early epochs of recovery for presenting suggestive ideas, are two rules that work wonders in rebuilding the higher life among those temporarily depressed.

The apparent miracles of new types of belief are readily explained if the relation of suggestion to surplus energy is once understood. Prominent as are these cases, they are less significant than the working of the same principle in normal people, in their periods of growing vigor. Natural suggestion, with its power of inspiration, comes to them in times of energy; it pushes them into a contact with nature by its propelling force. All men might feel its promptings if surplus energy were not so freely used in the pursuit of material ends or of social dominion. We get inspiration when we cut down our wants and isolate ourselves, not because these ends are bad, but because they exhaust energy. It is stored-up energy that brings on states of inspiration. We can, therefore, create inspiration just as we can avoid the thought of pain. In the reconstruction these two changes bring is the hope of religion and the promise of a better life.

CHAPTER XII

HISTORIC OR STATE RELIGION

XII

I have kept in the background the actual development of religion, because the thread of human progress is lost in a recital of confusing facts and present creeds. Our first task has been to outline the basal ideas on which religion rests. We must now bring these ideas into harmony with religion as we find it expressed in historic institutions and voiced by prevailing religious sentiment. Natural and historic religion, instead of being harmonious growths, seem to be antagonistic tendencies. They have little in common but a name. The causes of this divergence are not hard to find; and if they are once clearly presented, the conciliation of the two becomes possible, even if its realization is remote. The essential difference arises from the fact that natural religion is an expression of surplus energy, while historic religions have assumed their well-known forms under the pressure of deficit. Had the history of national resources been different, religion would have become, not an expression of sorrow, but of joy.

These evils and the race antagonisms they provoke made each nation a coherent group and forced men to subordinate themselves to the needs of the state. The duty of sacrifice was in its origin political, and becomes religious only because of the close union between the two. The fierce struggle for national independence evoked sacrifice just as it did bravery, and the two qualities grew together as national conflicts increased in violence and frequence. Sacrifice becomes a virtue only under the pressure of want, and must have as a background the presence of war, famine, disease and national disorder. Historic religion is state religion because it reflects the ideas imposed by race conflicts and emphasizes the virtues they bring forth.

We may well regard the historic and the prehistoric epochs as stages in economic development from which two types of religion have risen. By this I do not mean that there ever was a natural man of the kind Rousseau pictures, nor even a natural religion like that of the theologians. Both of these concepts present man as he would be in a naturally utopian environment, or in a developed economic régime. If we would picture with any accuracy the prehistoric man, we must strip away all traits acquired in this advanced régime and all political and moral advantages flowing from it. This process, if thoroughly applied, would give results so peculiar as to have little value. We cannot reconstruct or revive the natural man. To bring him back would be a loss, not a gain. Yet there are elements in this early situation so clear and striking that to neglect them would make history unexplainable and give a wrong interpretation to human nature. By making prominent the traits that survive, instead of emphasizing the details of the long epoch in which these traits arose, we falsify history and present an artificial man. But we do, by this means, reach the essence of man's progress. The description of a long series of events in many changing environments would obscure this progress and defeat our purpose. Natural characters reflect a single possible environment. This we should try to reconstruct, even if the effort yields a mere Utopia.

The essentials of this pictured prehistoric state should be thought of in terms of health rather than in those of welfare. Man's constitution shows that he is a long-lived being. For his development there must have been a period when the natural span of life was more fully realized than in the recent past. Disease in its present forms is a result of historic conditions. Especially is this true of the great epidemics that have so much shortened life. Filth comes mainly through overcrowding; contagious diseases could not have antedated it. When the world was sparsely populated and the natural surplus large, a mature old age must have been the general expectation. Infant mortality was doubtless large; but this would not have much influence on social organization if this dangerous period was followed by a long period of vigorous manhood. Old age would also, as with animals, quickly lead to death. The young and vigorous would thus set the pace and shape social and religious usages. Then youth and vigor were long and old age short; now, youth is but a passing moment and old age an enduring, hopeless epoch. With us the senile hand is on every institution and influences every social event. It is not to be wondered that religion has reflected this change and has become a thing of age and grief.

The economic conditions of early times also emphasized joy above sorrow. Nature was irregular in the bestowal of its gifts. Periods of abundance and want followed each other with great frequency. But when nature gave, it gave freely. Periods of plenty were free from worry. They became the occasions of great festivals that aided much in shaping early institutions. Memory dwelt on the joy of living during its best moments, rather than on the reviving of the evils incident to periods of want. Distress and woe must become chronic before they mold social thought. This can happen only after the social surplus has been appropriated by dominating groups. So long as all participate in the surplus their lives will be shaped by its pleasures. Chronic poverty is due to a pressure which could not have been felt before historic institutions deprived the poor of their share of the free gifts of nature.

Religion under these conditions becomes the inspiring uplift of life, not a preparation for death. It arose and expanded with the increased vitality of spring, with the freshening influences of outdoor life, with the songs and festivals of the harvest, with the sports and amusements of public gatherings, with the joy of victory and the pleasures of prosperity. Some of this religion has remained in a subdued form and has become a part of modern life; but most of it was crushed out in the struggle of later religions to reduce life to a simple moral basis. In the pagan times it still held a place, for morality had not yet been differentiated from public life. But to the Hebrew prophets it became idolatry, and was swept aside in the endeavor to secure a clearer concept of God, a purer morality and greater social justice.

Had economic conditions been normal and had a long, prosperous life been the reward of right action, the new morality might have been blended with existing social institutions. Each would thus have felt increased vigor. Health, prosperity, justice, morality and the joy of life could have been blended into a higher harmony, of which religion would have been the best expression. The economic shortcomings of the localities in which civilization arose did not permit this. Western Asia was in a state of physical decline during the period when its civilization was forming. A reduction of rainfall was coupled with a type of agriculture that wasted resources. Nation after nation became the seat of civilization, only to go down before the pressure of want brought on by reduced rain supply and bad use of the soil. The resort to irrigation gave only temporary relief, for in the end the crushing power of failing resources makes futile even the best of plans. A secondary result of these conditions was a constant unrest of nations with resulting feuds and wars. No nation can have a normal growth with poverty-stricken neighbors trying to displace it. War, therefore, became the glory of nations, and pillage was more honorable than industry. To these evils were added the great plagues arising from the increasing contact with semitropical regions. Famine, war and disease became scourges, making life so insecure as to seem worthless. With the terrors of death ever imminent, it was inevitable that religion should reflect the change. A future life and its rewards became the compensation for the trials and suffering bound up with present existence.

[186]

In the midst of these changes, and reflecting the ideas that sprang from them, the Jewish nation arose and became the mold in which modern religion took its form. Judea was an isolated valley with enough resources to create a national life, yet not large enough to resist invasion. The growth of commerce brought tropical diseases from which the land would have been exempt if the earlier isolation could have been preserved. But worst of all was the steady increase in the extent and duration of periods of drought. These led to famine and destitution, which became objects of anticipation and dread. Under these conditions men were powerless. The prophet had only to persist in his prediction of disaster to have some one of the great national evils — war, pestilence and famine — come to his aid and establish his reputation. It is hard to conceive of evils worse than those steadily augmenting during the period of Jewish history, or in which men could be more helpless. Morality could delay, but it could not prevent the inevitable downfall that the whole region had to face. The prophets chose the only road open to salvation. But even this could do no more than relieve the momentary pressure on individuals or on localities. The general decline and the growing disorder went on unabated.

The general demoralization of the Roman epoch

was the natural fate of regions thus afflicted. Declining resources, contagious disease and war could not but destroy the basis on which long life and prosperity depend, and take from people the accompanying joys of living. Roman history is that of an age when dominant races lived on plunder and pillage. Each military epoch exhausted the stored wealth of preceding years and forced the people into viler and more slavish conditions. Diminishing resources compel men to resort to exploitation and to shorten life by its oppressions.

The Christian epoch brought no permanent relief. It had to face the same economic conditions and be molded by them. In some respects it made matters worse; for the general expectation of an early millennium led men to accept evils that would have brought immediate revolt without the hope of the life to come. Christianity did not bring a new philosophy of life nor furnish the starting point for a revolt against oppression. It did not even lead to a revival of old morality, such as was to be found in the religion of the prophets. In its theology, the old philosophy of deficit had a stronger hold than with the pagan nations. The prophets were men from the country. They were inspired by the natural suggestion that goes with great vitality. The new leaders were men of the cities, with no natural background to arouse revolt against its misery and vice. The conditions they saw were to them an inevitable result of man's depravity; and they were led by this belief to an even worse view of life than their predecessors. Exploitation had no social traditions to check it, and disease baffled the knowledge of the day. Famine and pillage could end only in poverty. The consequent loss of national spirit demoralized men so much that their natural resistance to oppression failed to assert itself.

It is not surprising, therefore, that Christianity succumbed to this pressure and became the medium through which old ideas were strengthened and propagated. Sacrifice was ennobled, and the primitive thought of an atonement was so vividly presented that the sayings and spirit of Christ were dimmed. The church made no break in the continuity of the old social thought and life. It had no institutions other than those grafted on it from the heathen world, no philosophy that reflected its founder's thought. The power of defeat, the growing dread of death and the emphasis of sacrifice warped its institutions until they expressed the reverse of what Christ taught. Nor have organized revolts and secessions from the church affected much. Protestantism was a political and economic revolt from the South. The new school of theologians were more pronounced advocates of the old thought than were their predecessors. The breach between God and man was made broader and more formidable than ever. Pictures of future misery got a new emphasis, history was ransacked to show man's helplessness, sacrifice was extolled as the cardinal virtue, and hardship as the only road to morality and character.

This is the philosophy of deficit expanded and augmented. There was no break in the continuity of historic religion. Protestantism is merely its fulfillment and goal. The old grind of misery, with its resulting theory of life, was destined to persist until a new basis for civilization arose in the growing surplus of Northern nations. Germany and England were outside the region of drought and failing resources. With their rise a reorganization of political institutions began to conserve instead of destroy liberty, health and capital. This steady stream of prosperity has created new modes of thought and undermined the old philosophy of deficit so long the terror of mankind. Prosperity, liberty and coöperation furnish a principle more potent than the dread of want. When we accept it, we shall rebuild on safe foundations, and make religion a higher expression of manhood than it could become while state religions and ascetic morality suppressed the vigor, joy and freedom of normal life.

[190]

CHAPTER XIII

SOCIAL RELIGION

XIII

In the preceding chapter I have contrasted two types of religion. Both have a basis in objective conditions, and elements of each must be present in all organized religious manifestations. Natural religion — the religion of vigor and joy — springs out of the surplus of nature and the plasticity of youth. It shows itself where material conditions are stable and long life is the reward of effective action. Primitive religion in its social aspects was of this type. From it we can infer what would have been its force and character if growth had not been interrupted by the strenuous events of later times. Historic religion does not spring from these conditions of surplus, but from a deficit. The nations that were to shape religion lived in regions where resources were failing and disease on the increase. To these evils were added race hatreds and instability of government that brought on wars, with resulting pillage and destruction. Religion was forced to reflect these changes. In the regions where these evils were greatest, a body of doctrine and practice grew up that has since then been

o [193]

expressed in religious institutions. Drought, disease, war and other evils of a state of deficit being dominant in Western Asia while our religion was forming, we must turn to these regions to discover the forces that compelled religious thought to develop as it did. The lack of a clear demarcation between church and state forced religion to become a mere adjunct to patriotism and to express its needs. The difficulty of maintaining national independence led to a similar subordination of the individual to the state, and forced the emphasis of valor and self-sacrifice as virtues. The resulting changes in thought, feeling and education have passed on from age to age and from nation to nation with increasing emphasis, until they have colored all religious expression. Ages of failing resources have made men feel that life is not worth living, that virtue has no reward except beyond the grave.

Despite clearness and power, state religions, with their emphasis on individual sacrifice, have never been able fully to satisfy the religious instinct of men. There has been a constant tendency to revert to a natural religion in which joy, liberty and inspiration were prominent. This struggle has been especially keen in the Northern nations where stable economic resources enabled men to displace many of the sources of misery that depressed the Southern nations. Were state religion and natural religion to fight out the battle for supremacy in nations where the dominance of man over nature is nearly complete, there is little doubt of the outcome. Natural religion would assert itself and profoundly modify present religious institutions. But there is little likelihood of such a struggle. The contest will not be so much between these contestants as between them and another type of religious expression. State religion is a result of war and want: natural religion arises out of contact with the surplus and vigor of nature; social religion is quite as clearly based on the thought of peace and plenty. A religion of joy, a religion of sacrifice and a religion of service are contrasted ideals, each dominating in its own fitting circumstances.

The religion of service could have no better exposition than in the teachings of Christ. What we need is not to formulate a clear statement of it, but to find conditions and institutions to make it effective. Christianity in this sense is not an historic institution. It is an ideal that has fought a losing battle with state religions, encrusted in historic institutions and made vigorous by the failures of men in ages of disease and want. The sayings of Christ seem utopian even to those influenced by them. To the mass of men they are meaningless, because they are not impressed by such striking pictures as those enforcing a religion of sacrifice. To be a hero, to struggle for victory, to die for one's country, have vivid meaning. They give an impetus to activity which the truer but less picturesque ideas of service do not arouse.

It is difficult to associate Christ with a purely social religion because His teachings have been overshadowed by the striking events of His death. For this reason we do not see the fundamental opposition between what He taught and what His death has been made to teach. If Christ's doctrines had been handed down to us by a Plato instead of a Paul, or by one who knew only of His life and not of His death, Christ to us would be a social leader, preaching salvation only in terms of love, coöperation and service. Salvation through sacrifice, especially through a blood atonement, would be a repugnant doctrine from the dread of which He wished to free the world. There is nothing more paradoxical in history than the rise of the dogma that a gulf is placed between God and man, which can be bridged, not by love, but only by the death of one who strove to fill the gap in the other way. This glaring antinomy in religious thought must be removed before social religion can be put on a sound basis. If Christ's doctrine be that of salva-

tion through love, the path is open to reconstruct
religion in ways that meet modern needs. If this is
not His view, a vague, perhaps hopeless, epoch of
religious confusion must lie ahead.

Bible readers fail to realize the opposition existing between the accounts of Christ's life, teaching and aims
and those of His death. If the last chapters of each
of the gospels were omitted, if we could see Him as the
disciples must have seen Him before they were influenced by His death, we should certainly view Him
as a man who believed in humanity and expected its
elevation to purity and morality through love, peace
and service. A purer social religion could not have
been preached than that He presented. Such of His
sayings and parables as have reached us all emphasize
this view. Yet Paul, influenced more by His death
than by His life, drew from this life a meaning and
gave to it a theological setting that stands in strange
contrast to what must have been an earlier view of
His life and teaching. The disciples were rightly
offended with this presentation, until they were drawn
into the social atmosphere that made Paul and subse-
quently made the Christian church. I make this contrast, not to discredit Paul and the church, but to
explain them. Paul's interpretation was a social
necessity. On no other basis could the church have

grown. Yet, with all its force and clearness, this interpretation misrepresented Christ in many fundamental points and gave a renewed vigor to doctrines He opposed.

To see the truth of these statements the social conditions and mental attitude of Paul's age must be pictured. Centuries of famine, disease and war had broken down the national life of the peoples over which Rome ruled and had blotted out the hopes, moral and social, that had come from earlier times. A religion was needed, dissociated from prevalent failures and disasters from which there was no hope of relief. That the world is a place of misery is not a doctrine of Christian origin; it was but a commonplace thought in the age that gave birth to Christianity. Such also was the doctrine of a gulf between God and man. War, famine and other evils in this view come from God and are indications of His displeasure. To picture a new way of reconciling God was the only escape from these difficulties that harmonized with current religious thought. A hope was thus created that did wonders in an age when evil and fear were dominant. By itself Christ's social philosophy would have gone down in the chaos of universal ruin. Paul's hope and faith did what Christ's teachings alone could not have done. The Christian church under his guidance reconstructed society and made the modern renaissance of thought possible. Christ's death was thus of saving importance to the race. There is a practical groundwork for the doctrine of the atonement that cannot in the abstract be given it. His death raised humanity from the lowest position into which men could fall, and permitted a shifting of the base of civilization to other regions with stable institutions.

The early Christians were in the midst of the depressing events accompanying the downfall of civilization. The hopeless outlook forced on them the belief that a betterment must come from without and not from within this civilization. Who could believe in works at a time when every endeavor ended in dismal failure? Christ's resurrection turned men's thoughts away from their misery and awakened the hope of a speedy second coming through which evil was to be displaced and an age of peace and love inaugurated. With this new faith, every war, plague, famine or other disaster was taken as an indication of the end of the natural régime and the approach of the new epoch. The more the tribulations, the nearer the redemption. The passing of twenty centuries has changed this outlook. Civilization is no longer centered in regions of waning resources and of increasing misery. The new regions have no fear of drought and famine; disease has been checked and life prolonged. Civilization has overcome the obstacles that blocked its path in Western Asia. A long upward movement is in prospect, instead of the rapid plunge into ruin that seemed inevitable in the first century. We should alter our conception of Christ to fit this situation. The second coming will mark the fulfillment of the hopes of civilization, art and science, not their failure. The social philosophy of Christ will thus triumph over the cruder concepts of His death. The unity and peace of the world will come, instead of its destruction. The crucifixion was a temporary expedient which hastened the changes that make Christ's social ideals workable. Christ's life was for the world. His death was for His age and its civilization.

At the end of two thousand years the striking result of Christianity has been the shifting of civilization from the South to the North. The economic significance of this lies in the growing resources of the North in comparison with their decrease in the South. In the new region there was too much rather than too little rain; and a better food supply was afforded by the cereals of the North than by the root crops of the South. The North of Europe could not, however, have risen to its present commanding position without an impetus from the South. Had the Northern region been completely isolated, its rise would have depended entirely on its internal resources. Its civilization would have been limited to arts, foods and material of its own origin, and its people could scarcely have risen above a state of savagery. While the North had the climate that makes prosperity permanent, it had indigenous few of the crops or animals on which a great civilization depends. These were from Western Asia, or at least came north with Southern civilization. To an equally great degree did the arts, trades and ideas of civilized life come from the Southern races. These could not have developed in the cold North, or at least would have been absent for ages. Northern prosperity is thus a union of Northern resources and Southern arts, foods, animals, tools and culture. Had the two failed to blend, there would have been an insurmountable obstacle to the continuance of culture.

Only five regions had conditions favorable for great civilization: China, India, Western Asia including the Mediterranean basin, North Europe and America. India and China were already filled with a teaming population and had not in themselves the elements for further progress. America could not be reached, and probably could not have been utilized until after the transformations that the rise of civilization in

North Europe would make. America, even more strikingly than North Europe, was a land of resources. But it likewise lacked the adjuncts in native food, animals and arts that permit their utilization. The only hope of a permanent civilization lay in its transference to North Europe. The prospect of this would seem hopeless; for to the people of the South the Northern races seemed as savage as the Indians do to us. For ages Northern tribes had been pressing south, and with them in their natural state nothing but brutality could follow their dominance.

If the transference of civilization had not been accompanied by the rising missionary spirit of the early Christians, it is easy to picture what would have happened to Southern civilization. Its resources would have continued to fall off, the ravages of disease would have increased, and war would have become increasingly brutal and destructive. A situation like that in Arab countries would ultimately have arisen and have remained permanent. The rise and decline of Mohammedanism showed what could happen to any civilization that has its base in the dry regions of the South. Under these conditions, Christianity might have created a Spain, but it could hardly have done better. The dogmatism of arid regions would certainly have prevented the rise of science, and without it any amount of resources could yield nothing but failure.

The natural obstacle to the progress of civilization lay in a doubly contradictory situation. The only place where civilization could begin its rise must fail because of the niggardliness of its economic situation; the regions where its permanence was possible lacked the cultural conditions for its rise. The miracle of civilization consists in the solving of this contradiction by uniting abundant resources with the arts and culture making them available. This I believe is a fair interpretation of twenty centuries of Christian progress, measured by to-day's standards. Only when it is substituted for the defective view of the first century can Christianity be placed on a firm basis.

There are bound up in Christian thought two distinct plans of salvation. The orthodox view has the degenerate conditions of the Roman world as a background. It appeals to the emotional type of man these conditions produced. If instead of saying Christ died for sinners we say He died to redeem the degenerate, we put the problem of this religion in a scientific form. Its emotional awakening creates character and evokes motives, causing the spiritual to dominate over the degenerative forces of a world of deficit. It was this religion that gave new life to the Roman world and supplied the impetus carrying civilization from the pessimistic South to the optimistic North. It is almost a universal religion because degeneration is so widespread and its emotional psychology so deep-seated. It must, however, be regarded as a temporary necessity, approved as a last resort and not as a chosen plan. It does not reflect the religion of the normal man, nor does it manifest the social spirit of Christ's teachings. Another and purer religion lies in the background. This is obscured in the Old Testament by the devices of priests, and in the New by the enthusiasm of Paul's disciples. The normal life of a stabler civilization is helping us to reconstruct it and to put in practice doctrines distinctly Christ's. The Holy Spirit He promised is with us as the social spirit. In it we have a natural guide to conduct and an effective stimulus to coöperative action.

This view does not detract from the dignity and beauty of Christ's death, but adds to it. When He cried, "My God, why hast thou forsaken me?" did He regard the forsaking to consist in His physical death or in the failure of His social philosophy? If He were in earnest about His teaching, He could hardly have thought its failure of little importance, compared with His life. And yet the conventional view makes Him forget His gospel in His hour of agony and think of its pain. It will not wrench nor weaken the story of the Passion to set aside this interpretation, and to have Christ dread the cross, not because it meant a physical death, but because it would revive and seem to put His stamp of approval on a religion He condemned and hoped to replace. To die to save civilization would have had no meaning to the early Christians who felt keenly the need of a reconciliation with God. To us, however, the false light in which Christ let Himself be put by a striking death is but an exemplification of His doctrine of service. His real mission will be fulfilled by a second coming to which the first is but preliminary. Meanwhile the basis of enduring progress has been secured. In this we can not only participate, but can promote by the social service which His life so amply illustrates.

CHAPTER XIV

THE SOCIAL MISSION OF THE CHURCH

XIV

THE preceding discussion has revealed an economic environment and a body of psychic reactions that afford new principles of religious activity which should make religion an active force and give its plan of salvation a background worthy of consideration. Degeneration and regeneration are realities; the power to resist the one and to gain the other is equally real and must have a place in every scheme of social progress. A deficit of energy brings degeneration: a surplus of energy, evoking will power, leads to regeneration. Enthusiasm and missionary spirit come with the growth of physical vigor. We can expect it to develop a religious expression if the thought of redemption can be put in a social setting. As a plan of progress, religion emphasizes the incorporation of the weak into society. If the degenerate cannot be aroused, strengthened and made normal, if on the contrary he must be eliminated, religion will have no place in the utopia toward which we are moving. Progress by elimination and progress through redemption are opposing concepts, one of which must be proved wrong by the trend of events.

If Christians, adhering to an unsocial concept of religion, fail to show that redemption for the masses is attainable, they must not find fault if the ideal of an unsocial superman displaces that of service. The social plan of redemption will be tested in this century as the hope of personal salvation was tested by the facts and conditions of the first century. A new missionary movement is demanded in our age. To succeed, this must have the vigor and clearness of thought that Paul gave to the first extensions of Christ's influence. The impress of past centuries has put modern religion in as helpless a condition to meet present emergencies as the Jewish religion was in the first century. The work that Christ began could not be fully developed in the early centuries because of adverse economic conditions. It can, however, be successfully completed now because favorable environing conditions have replaced race antagonisms with a spirit of social coöperation. This has opened the road to social regeneration as contrasted with social elimination. To meet this new situation is the religious need of the day. Success or failure are alternatives that will make Christianity dominant or will displace it as an encumbrance to progress.

There are many analogies between the present situation and that which Christianity faced at its birth.

THE SOCIAL MISSION OF THE CHURCH

The present crisis, although of another character, is fully as grave as that of the first century. Disease, famine, war and failing resources made impossible an advance in civilization in the Southern regions, then its center. A new region must be opened up and new races must be elevated from barbarism into the position of standard-bearers of culture. To-day, we have no fear of war, famine, disease or failing resources. The advance in knowledge has guarded men against these evils; but it is none the less true that civilization must be extended to other regions and races, or it will go down as it did at Rome. Prosperity checks the birth rate and promotes race suicide to such a degree that if new races cannot be raised to take the place of those dying out, there will be a decline in civilization to the level existing before the rise of Christianity. All of the earlier missionary efforts will be in vain unless methods are devised to arouse new classes, races and nations with the same success with which our ancestors were awakened in earlier epochs by the prevailing forms of religious propagation. If laborers remain outside the church, if immigrants are not assimilated into our national life, or if we fail to do for Africa, India and China what the early Christian missions did for our German ancestors, a slow but certain death awaits the church, no matter what may be its success in other fields. No headway is possible unless there come modifications of attitude and doctrine that will make the church a force among races and classes it at present fails to reach.

Our condition can be most simply and clearly contrasted with that of the first century in terms of the economic stages of progress. In early times, men were in a pain economy. This means that their energies were much more fully directed to the avoiding of enemies and dangers than to the production of goods. The primitive man was weak in comparison with the energetic animals surrounding him. He had to escape from them rather than fight them. Fear was thus a dominant motive. Enjoyment came only in the intervals between the dangers that beset his path. These conditions and the mental attitude that accompanies them were exaggerated by the environment of the race during the period of Rome's decline. Disease, famine, war and unstable government tend to make fear prominent as a motive. It keeps the effects of these evils constantly before men and forces them to endure long epochs of suffering and want. Experience, history and long-standing psychic reactions all united in emphasizing the same facts and in creating the same mental atmosphere. To men molded by these conditions the early centuries of missionary endeavor were directed. The gospel of fear, then advanced, matched the conditions, the civilization and the thought processes with which men were familiar. The twentieth century, however, differs from the first in that a pleasure economy has displaced the pain economy then prevailing. The thoughts and activities of men are now turned toward the pleasures of life. Those activities have become supreme that help men to increase their joys. It is true the advance has not gone far enough completely to set aside want, war and disease; but at least enough progress has been made to protect most men from their evils. They seldom rise to the point where they disturb our regular activities and the flow of pleasurable goods that follow.

The movement in this direction has gone far enough to enable us to see both the advantages and the evils by which it is accompanied. The good lies in our security, our pleasures and our freedom from want and disease; the bad lies in the fact that the pursuit of pleasure does not arouse the energies nor concentrate them enough to keep men normal nor to make them progressive. Our economic wants do not awake men's activity in the forceful, direct way that the fear of enemies, of nature or of disease did in earlier times. A pleasure economy fails at the point where the older pain economy was most successful. Concentrated attention, quick and forceful action, a willingness to submit to discipline, a love of local usages and an enthusiasm for national ends came as a part of the regular reactions of a life controlled by danger and pain. The seeker for economic goods, freed from these long-standing evils, shows no such qualities. He is not as eager to work as he was to fight, nor will he submit to the industrial discipline he would accept without question if he were a soldier. He works carelessly, shows little desire for efficiency and will not limit his use of goods so as to preserve his health.

I do not wish to charge economic materialism with all the evils that are to-day becoming manifest. Our vice and crime are due to a degeneration that has its causes largely in the past. A pleasure economy would ultimately displace the tendencies that end in vice and crime. Its real evils do not lie here, but in the lack of concentration of activity that keeps men normal and thus tends to make the race progressive. We need strong, vivid ends for our activity as much as ever, and there is nothing in material wants that arouses them. If they come in our new civilization, they will appear in motives a pleasure economy has no tendency to promote.

The results of this failure of a pleasure economy to

arouse motives and to set definite ends clearly before men are reflected in the devices at present used to make men effective. Society still resorts to old methods to create discipline and to generate activity even when it relies on utilitarian motives to supply our economic needs. A compromise has been worked out by which the motives of a pleasure economy are supplemented by the driving power of the old régime, in the form of fear. Pain is not now prominent enough to concentrate men's energies; but fear, as contrasted with actual pain, has lost little of its force. It lies back of the discipline and concentration of energy now manifested both in individual and in national activities. The advanced nations seldom feel the miseries of war; yet the fear of war is the prominent motive in national effectiveness. Patriotism manifests itself in fortifying the Panama Canal and in building huge warships more readily than in conserving our forests or in lengthening human life. Each nation centers its activities on preventing a corresponding progress on the part of others and can be stimulated to extraordinary energy only by the constantly reappearing dread of foreign aggression. No political motive has arisen that will unite a nation and arouse its latent energies comparable with the effect of a foreign war or even the fear of one. Men who would not submit to an industrial discipline of ten hours a day will accept a much severer military discipline without a murmur. They have their characters built up by war or the fear of it in a way that no industrial program could enforce.

The present religious program also gets its power through fear. Without a vivid concept of future punishment the church would fail in the discipline it holds over its members. Its morality is largely built upon unseen relations that could not be made effective if fear were not a prominent motive. The same basis is found for the motives causing the accumulation of capital. Capitalism is often viewed as primarily the result of production on a large scale. Yet the discipline that creates qualities so definitely associated with it comes from saving, which in turn is evoked by the fear of future want. As soon as men lose their fear of poverty, they cease to save and will no longer submit to the discipline that makes capitalists a force and gives to industry its present form. Capitalism will die out much more readily through the loss of discipline that follows the cessation of saving than through any revolution its opponents may provoke. Nor are the socialists on any other basis than the classes they would displace. Class antagonism and the fear of oppression are as prominent elements in the discipline they evoke as is the fear of want among the capitalists, the fear of war among patriots or the fear of the future among religious people.

There is no discipline worth considering in education, in morality or in political life that is not the outcome of aroused fear. A physical emancipation from want has come, but no psychic emancipation from fear. Until we understand what this means we can get no measure of the changes that separate the first century from the twentieth. The concentration of energies is as important as ever; but no method of bringing it about or of creating a new form of discipline has yet been devised to replace the motives of fear. These are a psychic inheritance from the distant past, and they reflect an attitude hostile to future progress. Through the discipline of fear we may be able to hold our own, but never to escape from our present complex economy into a real peace economy where social motives instead of social antagonisms control. A peace economy must be more than a utopia of satisfactions. It must create a discipline more rigid than that of fear and give to men that concentration of energies which evokes their best powers. Society cannot become telic until our psychic powers are reshaped to meet present conditions. No amount of material progress can compensate for mental stagnation.

The economic basis of a peace economy is readily

[217]

understood, and is fairly well worked out. Economic wants generate efficiency, and efficiency demands co-operation. The three combined give us wealth and prosperity. The psychic reactions of men in a peace economy are hard to present, because so little advance has been made in breaking from the discipline that fear generates. It will seem like mere theory to offer a contrasted scheme, but there is no other way in which the needs of progress can be set forth. The first step is to realize that a peace economy does not demand a new group of psychic qualities, but merely a change in the dominance of qualities already formed. It would be a long, tedious process to make the changes involved, if they had to be created by evolution. If, however, the need is not a creation, but a change in the dominance of opposing groups of characters, the transference of mankind from a pain to a peace economy may be worked out in a relatively short period. Fear reactions are no more fundamental, no more deeply ingrained, than are the social impulses to which they stand opposed. The social life of men has run along parallel with their misery and fears, and both phases of psychic development have had a long period in which to grow. Primitive life shifted men from one group of conditions to the other, thus making the one group or the other, for the time being, dominant. We have thus a double psychic nature only single phases of which are manifested at a given time. An economy with a surplus tends to make us social; an economy of deficit arouses conflict and gives a dominance to pain reactions. The problem of social advance is thus on its material side to keep out of conditions of deficit and to get within the realm of surplus. On its psychic side, however, the problem is to keep our social nature dominant, and to suppress the fear reactions that nature has implanted. How then, in a realm like the present, partially of surplus and partly of deficit, can we make the social within us permanently dominant? — this is the problem that religion has to solve.

The starting point of this movement must lie in economics, because our economic interests give the most obvious motive for becoming social. Economic desires create interest in objects and the means of obtaining them. We may, therefore, say that desire leads to interest, and interest to knowledge and efficiency. The measure of knowledge and efficiency is twofold. Nationally, it is wealth; individually, it is health. As nations grow wealthy and men become healthy, we may be sure knowledge and efficiency are on the increase, and that a movement has been started in the direction of universal peace. National peace makes men wealthy; mental peace makes them

[219]

healthy. I make this contrast between the national and individual measures of progress because they are so often confused. By the old standard, men thought God was with them when they and their families prospered. This crude measure was good enough for primitive epochs, but to-day progress demands not individual wealth, but a large social surplus utilized for the good of society. As an individual measure, health is much better than wealth. Social health cannot exist without social wealth, but it may well exist without large fortunes. Moreover, when we have social wealth, the higher test of progress is health. This, measured statistically, means longevity. No test is so good as a low death rate and a long working period.

Health, wealth and efficiency are the basis of normal life. When we have these, we may be sure that degeneration, depravity, vice and crime will cease to be bars to social progress. A society, dominantly normal in its attributes, will thus replace the present one. In this a new group of social usages and traditions will grow up in favor of peace. The normal man is emotionally social. There is, consequently, in him a conflict between his social emotions and the habits, traditions, philosophy and logic impressed upon him by deficit and fear. All acquired traits have had their origin in the ages of deficit in which humanity has lived. They harmonize with the psychic fears these ages have generated. The motive for their upbuilding is lost when fear and pain cease to control men, and the crust they have formed in thought and habit is sure to be broken by the rise of social emotions. The conflict that disturbs the mental peace of men is between this crust of acquired tradition and the newly aroused emotions. The result is a regeneration, a new birth, or whatever name men apply to the radical reconstruction of thought and activity following the transference of dominance from emotions of fear and conflict to those of peace, harmony and joy. This change may be wrought in many ways, but the essence is a feeling of freedom from the thraldom of external codes and internal fears. From Paul to Christian Science, believers in a new birth emphasize the coming of mental peace and the freedom from the "law." Fear goes, and with its departure old habits and traditions lose their seemingly absolute character. New activities and modes of thought rise to replace them.

This is the essence of the mental reconstruction taking place when men become normal and hence emotionally social. If the analysis is correct, the "new birth" is not to be worked for. It will come of itself if men are made normal. Nor are we to regard it as the impress or gift of a higher power. The reconstruction and the peace it brings come because of what we eject from our lives, not from what is put in by outside powers. The break is in the economic and biologic determinism that control through deficit and fear, not through any inherent power they have over men. We are free when we make our own traditions and codes instead of submitting to external pressure and the dominance it imposes.

To make these facts effective in religion, a contrast must be made between the personal and social mission of the church. Each individual is born in a fear economy, and needs to have his fear of the future removed. The church does for him personally what saving does for the fear of want, or battleships do for the fear of foreign foes. The social mission of the church, however, is not to make men religious, but to make men normal. I say this consciously, because the religious awakening comes from within and can be wrought only by indirect means. The normal man is a religious man because his emotions are social, and because they clash with the economic and biologic régime imposed by heredity and external conditions. To make men normal is to start a train that leads to religious awakening. These indirect means will make more converts than the emphasis of fear. When such methods are employed, conversion will be a permanent change in mental attitude, and not a temporary upheaval. Missionary movements succeed only as they carry to new races and classes the underlying means for their betterment. Religion is contagious when these are secured. We can plow the land, but the fruit comes in its own way.

There is, however, one more step needed to make church work practical. The best evidence that religious movements are succeeding is that they make men live longer. A steady increase in the length of life has followed the spread of Christianity. When the average life of man has been increased to sixty years, the advantages of normal living will be overwhelming, and the strength of forward social movements correspondingly increased. Health is thus the test of normality, and the church can safely be sponsor for social movements that improve it. On this basis must the social program of the church be built. Many evils are beyond our present power to remedy. We cannot therefore make their removal part of a working program for the twentieth century. But the crimes against health are plainly within our control. We cannot make every one wealthy, but there is no need of poverty. Neither do we need to crush the life of children in factories, nor to lower the vitality of women by long working hours. A standard of living capable of maintaining health and welfare is not merely an ideal, but a perfectly workable plan. These and other economic reforms lie at the basis of all home missionary efforts, just as the health, security and happiness of other races is the essence of successful work abroad. Christianity needs, not preachers, but workers. Its supremacy can come only as civilization and culture are socialized and the economic world so transformed that the minimum of to-morrow's welfare will include more of health and comfort than the maximum of to-day's standards.

CHAPTER XV

THE SOCIALIZATION OF RELIGIOUS THOUGHT

XV

IF the social view of religion is to prevail, not merely is a new basis for religious activity needed, but also a radical modification in religious thought. As has been shown, thought has three stages: the traditional, or theological stage, the metaphysical or deductive stage and the pragmatic or social stage. In the first, social control lies in authority; in the second, it lies in the antecedents of actions; and in the third, it is in their results. While activity has in many ways passed over into the third stage, religious thought is still in the first and second stages. A religion of authority still makes a strong appeal; a metaphysical religion deducing its principles from a first cause or the ultimates of the universe also has great vitality. A social religion, however, seems to lack the clear, decisive elements giving force to authoritative and rational religion.

Authoritative religion has its basis in social tradition. It comes from the distant past and is colored by primitive modes of thought. Its appeal is largely to tradition, imitation and the feeling of submission that long periods of disaster and oppression impose. Its

[227]

basis, however, has been seriously weakened by the inroads of skepticism. In consequence, it would certainly die out if a union had not been made between it and the metaphysics of rationalism. God, as cause and creator, is the kernel and the goal of metaphysical thought. The gods of national tradition are thus displaced by the one God of infinite power and knowledge. This God is then united with traditional morality and made to give it an authoritative support. This metaphysical concept of God, coupled with traditional morality, viewed as a divine revelation, gives the basis of current religious thought. All the force of the first two stages of thought is thus given to religious concepts. Reënforced both by tradition and reason, and blended with a lofty idealism, they are hard to analyze, to dislocate or to transform.

Rational religion is strong where social religion is weak. Social religion lacks authority and has no rigid logic to make it effective. Social concepts grow; they are not made nor can they be coercively impressed. They are based on the agreements of past experience, verified by the current events in which all participate. The broader, deeper and more harmonious the social life of mankind is, the clearer do the social ideals stand forth and the more widespread is their influence. Social concepts appeal; they do not command. They arouse energy and direct activity; they do not repress, restrict nor define. Were all men normal, healthy and active, their force would be irresistible; for then men would be aroused by the same motives and struggle for the same ends. It is the opposition, the conflict, the degeneration, the differences in race, type, class and language that keep men so much isolated that common ideals and aspirations do not arise. Every barrier broken down between races, classes or languages leads to a blending of the thought and ideals of the united group.

The effect of this social process is apparent in many fields. From them we can see the way it will work in religion when the same process transforms, blends and unifies the various types of religion now contending for supremacy. A socialized world can no more have a dozen religions than it can have a dozen sciences in one field. As in medicine, there may, for a time, be a group of contending factions, but the growth of knowledge gradually forces them into unity, in which the half truths of each faction are transformed into the full truth of a united science. Arguments, proof and authority have little weight against the forces that are socializing thought, and thus bringing unity into religion as in other fields. The belief in one God results from a social tendency, not from a metaphysical

[229]

argument, nor from an authoritative tradition. So also there can be but one morality, and this will be made effective by the motives that prompt men to lead normal lives. Normality and morality have a common origin. Whatever raises the standards of normal life gives more force to morality and makes its rules more universal and coercive. A truly social morality will be more authoritative than any traditional code could be. At the same time, its basis will be so clear and attractive that no resistance to its dictation can arise. What men must do, and what they desire to do, will be so blended that no one will know which force determines his acts.

The present situation is confused by the way in which religious problems are faced. The early history of the race shows many religions, each with its own gods struggling for supremacy. There is also a marked contrast in primitive moralities, due to the concrete ways in which moral problems arose. In addition to this, the social philosophy of each nation began with generalizations about local conditions. These were transformed into universal philosophies without an adequate survey of the larger field to which they were applied. Each language was also formed by the situation in which the race using it arose, and its ideas reflect the experience of this race in its local position.

SOCIALIZATION OF RELIGIOUS THOUGHT

Religion shows the effects of all these difficulties, and judging from them there seems to be no unity to religious thought. Worst of all were the evils brought on by the subordination of religion to the state, for this made national contests appear to be religious and forced nations to increase their religious antagonisms so as to give a firmer background to national life. The natural process of blending religious ideas was blocked for ages by the patriotic aspirations of nations and differences in race and language. We thus seem to have religious conflicts where in reality none exist. Students of religion must be social before they are historical if they wish to see the beauty and harmony of religious concepts. Thought blends as nations and localities are united into larger areas. The common elements of many local situations become the ideals and standards of the larger group. In the end there can be but one economic group with the whole world as its habitat. Morality and religion must be reorganized so that they match this situation. When this happens there will be no opposition to their dictates nor any tendency to split up society into religious and moral factions. Unity, harmony and elevation are clearly visible goals in each of these fields. They will come as thought, activity and language are made to express general instead of local situations.

THE SOCIAL BASIS OF RELIGION

The situation that the early church faced had in it all these difficulties. The many national gods and religions created dissensions and opposition that were hard to placate. Differences in language also added much to the confusion, for each language crudely expressed the new religious thought. The statement of the apostle that "In the beginning, the Word was with God, and the Word was God" does not mean much to-day. The God concept has won out and the Word concept has blended with it or disappeared. The contrast, however, was real to the early Christians. They used different languages in which the God concept but partially developed, and as a result each group wanted to have the new ideas expressed in the concrete fashion to which they were accustomed. The blending of races, nations and languages always brings on these conflicts. Each group tries to defend its position by argument. The result is that religious controversy is aroused where no basis for it exists. Words and ideas cannot be defined and defended on any metaphysical basis. The problem of words is one of use, not of logic. We employ words until better ones are presented. They shift in meaning as the social background is more clearly defined and the area enlarged over which each language and group of ideas extend. The dictionary gives the best evidence of this growth. Words remain in use as long as they express ideas or adjustment. They drop out when more effective ways of expression are devised. Language tends towards a state where each thought has its word and each word expresses a distinct thought. As this goal is approached, controversy ceases and the common elements of thought are elevated into a secure position. Religion gains nothing by disputations that after all reflect only the defects of language or the imperfect socialization of thought.

That which has been true of the elevation of Christian thought in the regions dominated by it is equally true of the progress yet ahead by which the whole world will be united in one religion. The gods of India, China and regions yet to be religiously socialized will be displaced by the same process that has forced the Western world to accept a single supreme God. The disintegration of the older religious and moral thought will follow the coming of Western enterprise, education and science. The same blending of ideas and ideals will result that followed the changes in the Western world by which its unification and elevation were wrought out. To alter Eastern religions means to wipe out Eastern disease and to bring security, prosperity and education to regions that now lack them. One God will come with one economic system, one type of government, one science and one literature. The unifying forces are active in all these fields. They are delayed by argument and controversy. Our interest should lie, not in getting this inevitable unity, but in making it express in its various fields the highest thoughts that life, vitality and genius can attain.

The most difficult of all religious concepts to socialize is that of God. The early Gods were national and were associated with the power and grandeur of nations, or they were a protection against primitive fears. In both cases the demand is for a powerful master who protects and upbuilds. From these, thought advances readily to the concept of God as creator and judge. They presuppose the same dominance of God over nature and man as was accepted by the earlier religious thought. A rigid group of divine attributes is predicated from which all else is derived. Coupled with revelation, this view presents a God of authority and thus gives a background for a moral code unchangeable and inflexible, because of divine origin.

A social concept of God loses this definiteness. It cannot be made the basis of argument, and it lacks the authority that makes the earlier concept so satisfying to nations in conflict and to individuals in sin and despair. To make its basis clear and to show how it grows we must first think in terms of a united society from which discord and fear have been banished. Social forces now suffice to create the peace and harmony that to earlier races seemed only possible through external coercion. In such a society God will be transformed so as to reflect the thought stages of each individual in his development. There are many social concepts of God, but between them there is no opposition. The change follows the assent in thought that comes with social progress. It comes to the individual as he passes from youth to maturity, from ignorance to knowledge, from poetry to prose, or from depressed to exalted mental states. There is no real opposition between a pantheistic concept of God and a unitarian concept, nor between them and a telic concept. Change the thought of a man and he will alter his concept of God from one basis to the other without conflict or argument. As society progresses and as the men who compose it become more normal, the same concept will be held by all at maturity. Every one in his development will go through all the epochs of thought development out of which this higher concept has arisen. The social concept of God is a blend of all the views of Him that appeal to men in any stage of their progress. The clearer and more definite each of these elements is, the more perfect and elevating is the joint result.

How this process works in places where discord, fear

and argument present no obstacles is to be seen more clearly in other social concepts that have been put on a stable basis. The most social of all ideals is that which man holds of woman. He sees woman, not as she is, but as he pictures her. This vision is due to the many ways in which the beauty of woman is presented. If one view of woman were declared orthodox and all others opposed or excluded, the ideal of woman would be lowered and its power to restrain men correspondingly reduced. There is no opposition to the various views of women given by art. They blend into a composite picture and create a powerful social force to restrain the brutality and passion of men. So is it with the concept of God. Gods are in opposition only in national contests. They are made diverse by every struggle or argument into which men enter. Lift the obstacles that struggle and argument impose, and the unifying tendency becomes supreme. God now reflects all the moods and aspirations of men and from them an ever nobler concept emanates. The higher the level of thought, the more is His unity and glory reflected in it.

The socializing of religion is not a project for the future, but a process already well under way. Few realize that we have a modern gospel that is more effective, even if less authoritative, than the older gospel from which it sprang. The hymn book is the most inspired part of religious literature. This is due to the fact that its contents are the fittest survivals of modern endeavors to arouse religious enthusiasm. No one hymn contains all the truth, and each hymn contains some error or at least some defect in its viewpoint. As a basis for authoritative statement they would be sadly wanting, and yet when a congregation sings a dozen hymns, all are elevated in spirit by the united effect of the service. Hymns blend so that the joint effect is that of the best element in each of them. This does not make rigid theology, but it arouses effort. It makes men social and creates a feeling of unity and a spirit of coöperation. Poetry has also been effective in promoting a social view of religion and in giving to God qualities that appeal to men. Even where the poet's concepts have lacked some of the higher attributes, his ideal of God has done much to keep men religious. A religion of nature is better than a religion of strife. The poet has dwelt nearer to God than the theologian and felt more completely His impress. There is no opposition between the various religious concepts of literature any more than there is in the hymn book. They blend and elevate, and thus stand in contrast to the dogmas that disrupt and depress.

In these and other ways a natural religion has been formed that is a religion of appeal in contrast with a religion of authority. Social religion cannot furnish premises for argument nor can it put restrictions on conduct. It arouses what is in man and gives a stimulus to activity. Authority suppresses; nature evokes, animates and unifies. The passing from the discord of primitive life to modern social unity weakens authority and tradition, but the losses thus sustained are more than made good by the uplift coming through freedom, vigor and telic activity. The road from strife to peace runs also from restraint and servility to inspiration, hope and faith. Authority suppresses what inspiration evokes. The two are opposing phases of religious progress, one of which must disappear before the upward movement of modern thought.

The feeling in favor of authoritative religion comes largely from the belief that it furnishes the only adequate foundation upon which the moral code can rest. What is there to put in the place of the ten commandments is a question put with earnestness by many who fail to see any other basis for a moral code. The reasoning of the metaphysician has the same thought in the background. He believes that in proving the existence of a God he is saving morality from the quagmire into which utilitarianism and other inductive schemes of morality would put it. Deductive thinkers are primarily moral and not religious teachers. They think that sound

morality must have some antecedent principle or sanction. The moral imperative was nearer to Kant's
heart than other principles, and this basis of morality
he believed he had saved from the destruction which his
critical method wrought against other dogmatic principles. Nor has the moral attitude of the leaders of
science been different from that of philosophical
teachers. The one thing they have feared has been
that in the general destruction science was making
morality would suffer because no new basis had been
given it. Herbert Spencer broke in on the plan of his
philosophy and published the "Data of Ethics" out of its
order because he felt that a crisis in morality had been
brought on by the inroads science was making on traditional beliefs. He too wanted to find an antecedent
principle from which morality could be derived, and felt
as keenly as did Kant that without some such support
morality would degenerate. This unanimity of opinion
in favor of a morality that depends on antecedent principles makes it hard to present a morality based on its
subsequent effects. The change in thought must, however, be made if morality is to be transformed from a
personal to a social basis. Social morality gets its
force from its consequences; it has no antecedent principle from which it is derived nor any authoritative
sanction by which it is enforced.

THE SOCIAL BASIS OF RELIGION

To present clearly the social basis of morality a contrast must be made between culture and morality. Civilization and culture are carried along and improved by objective means. Cultural attitudes are acquired and come to each individual not as a part of his heredity, but from his education and environment. Culture and civilization survive even if the race that embodies them goes down. There has been a series of culture-bearing nations, each imparting its civilization to the next, but not its physical heredity. Our culture is not due to our racial ancestors, but to Greece, Rome and other ancient civilizations. Culture is thus objective and may exist along with a decline in physical traits. In fact, race suicide and culture are so intimately connected that the one rarely exists without the other. Morality, however, has race perpetuation as its end and test. The test of morality is not happiness and culture, but increased vigor and longevity. The test of vice, on the other hand, is decreased vitality and early death. "The wages of sin is death" is an old observation and as true to-day as ever. In favor of morality increased efficiency, vigor and longevity are always working. Against vice elimination is active. The moral is therefore that which gives vigor, while vice is that against which elimination is at work. Morality is therefore not made by an argument nor derived from an antecedent principle. It is not even an intellectual act, but the result of evolutionary and eliminating forces. Where a new morality is forming there is a modification of type due to the elimination of the vicious and the growing vigor of the virtuous. Contests in morality are a struggle between types each striving to make its views the social standards of the community. Morality is built up around the family as a center and it commands the specific things that preserve and elevate it. The improved family becomes a type, and the group struggle that follows is the basis of morality.

This can be plainly seen in present moral struggles, of which the temperance problem is an illustration. Mothers want to preserve their children and rear them with increased vigor and longer life. The saloon is an obstacle to this that must be displaced in the fight for family preservation. Temperance adds to life and vigor. The use of alcohol reduces both. In every community where this opposition exists there is a type formation which ends in a contest between the abstainer and the drinker. Back of all arguments are these racial differences with a struggle and a class differentiation that ends in the domination of one faction. Social differences may be settled by reason and compromise; moral differences lead directly to struggle and coercion. The forces back of morality are thus not reason and

R [241]

authority, but the increase of vigor and the elimination of the unfit. We need look no farther than this to find the basis of the coercion that moral codes exercise. Attractive morality represents only the early stage of moral progress before differences in type are clearly manifest. Repressive morality is sure to follow, because it is the only means by which social unity can be maintained. The family must be strengthened, even if it be at the expense of culture.

The process, however, does not stop here, but is made social by a change in attitude towards the means by which family life is maintained. Attractive morality and coercive morality are remedial and not constructive ; they induce people to leave the bad or prevent them from securing it. Social morality is constructive and displaces the evil instead of keeping men from it. All evil is specific and local. It has definite economic and social conditions as its antecedent. These can be attacked and removed. When a community attains this viewpoint, it thinks less of coercion and more of constructive measures that free society from long-standing and deep-seated barriers to a moral uplift. Constructive morality is, however, both attractive and coercive. Every public measure to remove disease, degeneration, vice and crime must be general in its application and hence coercive ; yet the coercion is not exercised against individual acts, but against bad social conditions. So also is it attractive; yet the appeal is not to personal happiness, but to public welfare. Social morality thus has in itself all the elements for its upbuilding. It does not need antecedent tradition, superior authority nor external sanction.

Natural religion and morality make two inherent constituents of social religion. Both are to be found in the earliest religions, and they have continued as prominent elements ever since. A religion of appeal and a coercive morality arouse men and elevate social religion. The third element is of later origin. No name has been given it, since it has appeared under such different aspects that it seems to have no unity. To bring its constituents into closer harmony, I shall call it Social Anticipation. It might be called utopism, but this would give it an unreality that it does not deserve. We think of utopias as artificially constructed societies so different from the present that to enter them human nature must be modified and society revolutionized. Such radical reconstructions reveal only in part the real forces back of social anticipation. All to-morrows are the basis of hope and the generating ground of faith. Normal men modify to-day's acts by the faith and hope that needs to-morrow for their fulfillment. The future is in the present and thus helps to construct itself.

In religion these anticipations become the doctrine of a Messiah, a looked-for leader who will displace despair and defeat with courage and accomplishments. The origin of this anticipation is obscured by the claim that the predictions about Christ did not arise out of a natural inclination to seek for help and an equally natural belief that it would come. Yet nothing is plainer than that the depressed, hopeless condition of the Jewish nation must lead to such anticipations. Human hopefulness revolts against failure; it sets up goals to strive for. National ideals are anticipatory, and from them come some of the strongest motives that elevate humanity and give stability to political institutions. It is equally clear why after the death of Jesus, the Christ ideal should become prominent. Christ was to return immediately and in great glory. All the failures of the past were to be wiped out in the reconstruction and redemption He was to bring. The Christ of the future thus displaced the Jesus of history in the thought of the early Christians; with the change came hope in the place of despair. All this was a natural movement which elevated and strengthened the church until it changed its basis from anticipation to tradition. It thus became an authority that depressed, instead of a hope that strengthened. The old spirit and enthusiasm would come again if this process were reversed. We can have an upbuilding religion only when it looks to the future and arouses faith in human betterment.

The crust of religious tradition and the doctrine of total depravity have kept the social anticipations of modern races from assuming a religious form. Religion separated from national aspirations has remained static. The tendency towards social anticipation has been active in forming utopias and in creating ideals about the natural man and the brotherhood of men. The democratic spirit has done much to arouse anticipations of social reconstructions which blend and elevate humanity into a harmonious whole. The growth and stability of modern nations has also helped to turn men's attention to the future. Each nation has bright hopes of what is to come and expects an increase in power and influence that will transform and elevate the whole world. To-day anticipation is largely centered about socialistic schemes and gives them vitality. Socialism is a combination of an economic program of reform and of an ideal reconstruction of society that is to follow. With its present emphasis on class struggle it is antagonistic to religion; but when class struggle has disappeared and the material obstacles to social progress are surmounted, social anticipation will be more prominent. Religious and social aspirations will then harmonize. Socialism will go the road of previous reforms. As the economic

[245]

program for which it stands is worked out or displaced by a better one, the social background will blend with other movements of a similar nature and lead to a religious upbuilding. All progress starts with a definite scheme of economic reform coupled with new hope of social reconstruction. The economic part of the program depends for its success on definite changes. When these are made, there is a residue of social anticipation which unites with earlier anticipations to create higher social ideals. The same anticipation which shows itself in national life, in political reform and in socialism is also beginning to show itself in city life. This new unit about which social interests grow unites a program of improvement with anticipations of a higher social life. City planning, health and prosperity give a new direction to social ideals which in the end will be transformed into a religious movement to reconstruct what is within man as well as what is about him. The new City of God will not only be well planned, healthy and prosperous, but will also be the center of spiritual aspiration.

More powerful than any of these hopes and a complement to them is the thought of bodily and mental evolution as voiced by the eugenic movement and the disciples of a superman. Like other reforms, they start with a program that makes them antagonistic to religion.

SOCIALIZATION OF RELIGIOUS THOUGHT

This especially is true of the superman concept, which has been made the base of a self-centered morality. There will be a direct clash between social morality and the unsocial morality at present associated with the concept of a superman. The conflict, however, is with the two types of morality and when social morality shows its superiority, the thought of a superman will survive the defeat of its morality. The Christ ideal is the superman viewed socially. Christ is one type of leader for the human race in its ascent, physical, mental and religious. The other type is the self-centered egoist who moves up through the elimination he creates. The contrast between progress by redemption and progress by elimination will be amply illustrated in the struggle between these two views. Both, however, contain social anticipation in a clearer and more vivid form than any antecedent social movement. Out of this transformation a movement in thought is coming that will force religion to discard traditions and dogmas that separate it from other social ideals. The blending of all social aspirations is but a matter of time. When it comes, social religion will have its full growth and be the expression of the forces that upbuild men and make social thought dominant.

THE following pages contain advertisements of books by the same author or on kindred subjects

AMERICAN SOCIAL PROGRESS SERIES

Edited by SAMUEL McCUNE LINDSAY, Ph.D.

Professor of Social Legislation, Columbia University
and Director of the New York School of Philanthropy

A series of handbooks for the student and general reader, giving
the results of the newer social thought and of recent scientific
investigations of the facts of American social life and institutions.

1. ## The New Basis of Civilization

By PROFESSOR S. N. PATTEN, Ph.D., LL.D., University of
Pennsylvania

Cloth, 12mo, $1.00 net; by mail, $1.12

2. ## Standards of Public Morality

By ARTHUR TWINING HADLEY, Ph.D., LL.D., President
of Yale University

Cloth, 12mo, $1.00 net; by mail, $1.12

3. ## Governmental Action for Social Welfare

By PROFESSOR JEREMIAH W. JENKS, Ph.D., LL.D. Cornell
University

Cloth, 12mo, $1.00 net; by mail, $1.12

4. ## Misery and its Causes

By EDWARD T. DEVINE, Ph.D., LL.D., Columbia University

Cloth, 12mo, $1.25 net; by mail, $1.36

5. ## Social Insurance

A Program for Social Reform

By HENRY R. SEAGER, Professor of Political Economy in
Columbia University

Cloth, 12mo, $1.00 net; by mail, $1.12

PUBLISHED BY

THE MACMILLAN COMPANY

64-66 Fifth Avenue, New York

BOOKS OF RELATED INTEREST

On City Government

The American City

By DELOS F. WILCOX, Ph.D.

"In the 'American City' Dr. Wilcox . . . has written a book that every thoughtful citizen should read. The problems of the street, the tenement, public utilities, civic education, the three deadly vices, municipal revenue and municipal debt, with all their related and subsidiary problems, are clearly and fully considered." — *Pittsburgh Gazette.*

6 + 423 pages, 12mo, cloth, leather back, $1.25 net. Citizens' Library

Great American Cities

Their Problems and their Government

By DELOS F. WILCOX, Chief of the Bureau of Franchises, of the Public Service Commission for the first District, New York

A detailed account of present conditions in the half-dozen largest cities of the country, including Chicago.

Half leather, 12mo, $1.25 net

On Industrial Legislation

Some Ethical Gains through Legislation

By Mrs. FLORENCE KELLEY

The book has grown out of the author's experience as Chief Inspector of Factories in Illinois from 1893 to 1897, as Secretary of the National Consumers' League from 1899 till now, and chiefly as a resident at Hull House, and later at the Nurses' Settlement, New York.

Cloth, leather back, 341 pages, 12mo, $1.25 net. Citizens' Library

On Charitable Effort

How to Help

By MARY CONYNGTON, of the Department of Commerce and Labor, Washington

Not only is the professional charity worker often in need of advice as to the best methods of investigation, administration, etc., but the non-professional worker, with his zeal unrestrained by special training, is even more emphatically in need of such guidance as this sound and competent book gives.   *New edition, cloth, 12mo, $1.50 net*

PUBLISHED BY

THE MACMILLAN COMPANY

64-66 Fifth Avenue, New York

The Development of Thrift

By MARY W. BROWN, Secretary of the Henry Watson Children's Aid Society, Baltimore

"An excellent little Manual, a study of various agencies, their scope and their educating influences for thrift. It abounds in suggestions of value." — *Chicago Inter-Ocean.*

Cloth, 12mo, $1.00 net

Friendly Visiting Among the Poor

By MARY E. RICHMOND, General Secretary of the Charity Organization Society of Baltimore

"A small book full of inspiration, yet intensely practical." — CHARLES RICHMOND HENDERSON.

Cloth, 16mo, $1.00 net

The Care of Destitute, Neglected, and Delinquent Children

By HOMER FOLKS, Ex-Commissioner of Public Charities, New York City

CONTENTS. — Conditions prevalent at the opening of the Nineteenth Century; Public Care of Destitute Children, 1801–1875; Private Charities for Destitute Children, 1801–1875; Removal of Children from Almshouse; The State School and Placing Out System; The County Children's Home System; The System of Public Support in Private Institutions; The Boarding Out and Placing Out System; Laws and Societies for the Rescue of Neglected Children; Private Charities for Destitute and Neglected Children, 1875–1900; Delinquent Children; Present Tendencies.

Cloth, 12mo, $1.00 net

Constructive and Preventive Philanthropy

By JOSEPH LEE, Vice-President of the Massachusetts Civic League

CONTENTS. — Essence and Limitations of the Subject; Before 1860; Savings and Loans; The Home; Health and Building Laws, Model Tenements; The Setting of the Home; Vacation Schools; Playgrounds for Small Children; Baths and Gymnasiums; Playgrounds for Big Boys; Model Playgrounds; Outings; Boys' Clubs; Industrial Training; For Grown People; Conclusion.

Cloth, 12mo, $1.00 net

PUBLISHED BY

THE MACMILLAN COMPANY
64–66 Fifth Avenue, New York